LIVE LOUD
BREAKING FREE FROM SILENT CHRISTIANITY

ANTHONY VARGAS

ISBN: 979-8-9936947-2-6

Printed in the United States of America

First Edition

Unless otherwise indicated, all Scripture quotations are taken from the **Holy Bible, New International Version® (NIV).**

NIV® Scripture quotations are from the **HOLY BIBLE, NEW INTERNATIONAL VERSION®. NIV®. Copyright** ©1973, 1978, 1984, **2011 by Biblica, Inc.®** Used by permission. All rights reserved worldwide.

Scripture marked **ESV** is taken from **The Holy Bible, English Standard Version®. Copyright © 2001 by Crossway**, a publishing ministry of Good News Publishers. Used by permission. All rights reserved.

All emphasis added within Scripture quotations is the author's unless otherwise noted.

For more resources, visit: *AnthonyVargas.org*

Contact: *Anthony@youthpastortips.com*

To my wife, Bailee, your faith in Jesus and your love for me have shaped this book in ways words could never capture.

We're called to be the light of the world—not just on Sundays, but in our everyday lives. Anthony Vargas lives that truth boldly. There's no one better to write a book about living out your faith with courage and conviction. Drawing from years of ministry and a heart for people, Anthony gives us a powerful call to action: share Jesus wherever you are. *Live Loud* is more than a book—it's a challenge to live unashamed, to make your faith visible, and to leave a lasting legacy that points others to Christ. Read it, live it, and then pass it on. The world needs believers who will live loud for Jesus!

—Brian Mills, Senior Pastor, Together We Church

Every once in a while, there needs to be a book published that reminds us 'ordinary Christians' of our calling to share our faith. I am so grateful that my friend Anthony Vargas has faithfully crafted a book that challenges and equips us to have the courageous voice that bears witness of the hope that is in you. *Live Loud* will help Christians young and old rise above the fear that keeps us silent, so that we may share the hope that makes us loud.

—Brent Crowe, PhD, President of
Student Leadership University

Our world needs bold, authentic faith more than ever. In *Live Loud*, Anthony Vargas calls believers out of comfort and into courage. This book is a passionate reminder that following Jesus was never meant to be done in silence. Get ready to be inspired, encouraged, and challenged wherever you are on your spiritual journey. Vargas writes as a thought leader, pastor, and true practitioner—modeling through his leadership and life what it means to live loud.

—Dr. Derik Idol, Executive Director of the Center for Youth
Ministry, Liberty University

As long as I have known Anthony Vargas, his passion has been sharing Jesus. In *Live Loud*, Vargas exposes the fears and excuses that often keep Christians silent in their witness. Using Scripture and giving practical steps to help share the gospel in natural ways, Vargas helps every believer understand their role in evangelism. I've watched him for years live out the message of this book, and I'm so glad he finally put his heart on paper. This is a book you will want to read - and then go live.

—Jarrett Stephens, Senior Pastor at Champion Forest Baptist Church and Author of *The Always God: He Hasn't Changed and You Are Not Forgotten*

Anyone who calls Jesus Christ their Lord and Savior is called to share the gospel, but Anthony carries a unique anointing to help the next generation step boldly into that calling. I've witnessed his impact on students across America, and I've personally benefited from his ministry as my own son now proclaims the gospel with courage in open-air settings. Anthony is a true evangelist, one who brings gospel truth to a gospel-hungry generation.

—James McKinney Pastor and Author of *Navigating the Teenage Dating Years: A Biblical Roadmap for Parents*

Anthony Vargas is a passionate leader with his finger on the pulse of a coming generation. And in a changing world where quiet belief is often thought to be the new kindness and consideration, Anthony gives a great challenge to embrace the Christian calling toward personal evangelism. Having known him for years, I have seen these passionate words, Anthony has written on these pages, being lived out daily in the areas of his life. This book will be a great encouragement, challenge, and resource to all Christ-followers who want to grow in our calling to share the good news of God's grace with the world around us.

—Dr. Connor Bales, Senior Pastor of Quail Springs Baptist Church and Author of *Counted Worthy*

Anthony is passionate about the Gospel and active in getting it to those in need. This book communicates that passion. *Live Loud* is a simple, straightforward, practical, compelling approach to evangelism that is refreshing, conversational, and accessible to every believer.

—Todd Sanders, Oklahoma Baptists Falls Creek Program Director and Youth Ministry

Convicting, Inviting, Courageous......these are a few of the emotions that are awakened as you walk through *Live Loud*. Anthony opens the arena for all of us that follow Jesus to be soul winners. The time is now. This is a much needed resource that can motivate a generation.

—Jay Barbier, Tennessee Baptist Mission Board

You don't have to be around Anthony Vargas long to discover that is a guy who clearly loves Jesus and wants to make him known. That why I'm excited about *Live Loud*. The book is not born out of a theoretical approach to sharing Jesus with others. It comes from a place of Anthony's life-long personal growth with how to love others well and make Jesus known. The real-life confessions and experiences strengthen the practical suggestions on how we all can break free from silent Christianity.

—Chris Trent, Next Gen Catalyst, Georgia Baptist Mission Board

There are professional Christians who give us their writings, and then there are faithful practitioners who give us their heart. Anthony is the latter. I know this because he's one of my closest friends. I've served alongside Anthony and done enough life with him to know that whatever he does-it works. And if you're ready to move beyond simply "growing" into becoming an evangelist (a timeline we never see in the New Testament church) and step into being one now, this book is for you. Because obeying God's call to share isn't just a command-it actually works.

—Dane Leake, Central Student Director/Student Pastor,
Rolling Hills Community Church

Anchored in Scripture, *Live Loud* is a powerful resource for anyone longing to see lives transformed by the gospel of Jesus Christ. Anthony Vargas reminds the reader that the normal, everyday Christian is the chosen means of spreading the hope of eternal life. Its Christ-centered wisdom and practical examples will inspire readers to boldly embrace the call to share their faith.

—Andrew Black, Senior Pastor, Hopewell Baptist Church

Anthony Vargas doesn't just talk about living loud, he models it. This book captures his passion to help everyday believers find their voice and courage again. It's honest, practical, and deeply needed for the Church today.

—Dr. Jason Mick, Executive Pastor, United City Church

Anthony delivers a much needed wake-up call to the Church. *Live Loud* is more than a message, it's a movement to shake off comfort and boldly proclaim Jesus. Anthony reminds us that the Gospel is urgent and eternity is too real for us to stay quiet. If you've ever felt the tension between fear and obedience, this book will stir your heart toward action.

—Brian Preston, Senior Director of NextGen,
BattleCreek Church

FOREWORD

I've had the privilege of preaching the gospel for over twenty years to countless students, leaders, and churches across the nation. And if there's one thing I've learned, it's this: the Church doesn't have a message problem, it has a volume problem.

Most Christians believe the right things, sing about the right Savior, and gather in Jesus' name every week. Yet somewhere along the way, too many of us have learned to live our faith out in silence. We've grown comfortable keeping silent about the very news that saved our souls.

Jesus told His followers, *"What I tell you in the dark, speak in the light. What you hear in a whisper, proclaim on the housetops"* (**Matthew 10:27**).

Ultimately, Jesus didn't die on the cross boldly and publicly for us to live our faith cowardly and secretly. When it comes to the Good News, the Church can't be silent. We must proclaim it boldly!

That's why this book matters so much.

In *Live Loud: Breaking Free from Silent Christianity*, my friend Anthony Vargas issues a timely, Spirit-filled call for believers to turn the volume back up. This isn't just another inspirational read—it's a battle cry. It's a wake-up call to a generation of Christians who know the truth of the gospel but have forgotten the urgency of sharing it.

Anthony doesn't write from a place of theory; he writes from the trenches of ministry. His stories prove what I've seen again and again: God moves most powerfully through ordinary people who are simply willing to obey. You don't need a microphone, a platform, or a theology degree to change eternity. You just need a heart that beats with passion for Jesus and a mouth willing to speak His name.

Every chapter of this book carries a mix of conviction and encouragement that's rare to find. It exposes the lies that keep us quiet—fear, apathy, insecurity—and replaces them with biblical truth and bold confidence in the Holy Spirit. It's honest, it's challenging, and it's full of hope.

One of my favorite lines from Anthony's writing sums it up well: *"We weren't saved to sit in silence; we were saved to be sent."* That's it. That's the heart of the Great Commission. That's the kind of faith our world is desperate to see again, a faith that refuses to hide behind comfort, chooses obedience over convenience, and truly believes that eternity is real and that Jesus is worth everything.

So, as you read this book, I want to challenge you: don't just agree with it—act on it. Let it stir something deep in your spirit. Let it push you beyond fear and into faith. Let it remind you that your voice matters, your story matters, and your obedience matters more than you could ever imagine.

Because somewhere today, someone is waiting to hear what only you can say. All around you, every single day, people need to hear about Jesus.

My prayer is that *Live Loud* will awaken a new boldness in the Body of Christ. May the Church refuse to keep silent about the greatest news. When believers rediscover their voice and get loud, communities change, families are restored, and Heaven gets crowded.

It's time for the Church to rise up again and begin to obey the command of sharing the gospel.

— **Shane Pruitt**, **National Next Gen Director,**
North American Mission Board and Author of *9 Common*
Lies Christians Believe, **Calling Out the Called,** **Revival**
Generation, **and** *Not My Jesus*

CONTENTS

CONFESSIONS OF A SILENT CHRISTIAN

It happened in the most ordinary place—Hobby Lobby.

If you've ever been inside one, you know it's the land of endless throw pillows, inspirational signs, and enough fake greenery to trick you into believing you live in a rainforest. My wife was in her happy place, casually weaving through aisles of farmhouse décor like she was in a museum exhibit.

Meanwhile, I was in my usual role: professional cart driver.

Somewhere between "Bless This Mess" signs and a clearance bin of fall candles, I found myself scrolling halfheartedly through my Bible app. And then it happened—I spotted him.

A worker standing there by himself. No one around. No customers in sight. He wasn't rearranging shelves or pretending to look busy. He was just available. If evangelism had a giant neon sign, this was it.

I felt the Spirit nudging me. Say something. Share. Start a conversation.

It could've been simple. A "Hey man, how's your day?" or "Can I pray for you?"

But instead, my brain hit the panic button.

And oh, the lies came rushing in:

- "They don't want to hear this."
- "I'll just make it awkward."
- "What if I don't have the right words?"

It was like Satan himself had joined me in aisle seven whispering,

"Stick to browsing the candle scents, champ."

I didn't say a word. I stayed quiet. And in that moment, fear won.

It wasn't that I didn't love Jesus. It wasn't that I didn't care about the person in front of me. I did. But the voice of fear felt louder than the voice of faith. I convinced myself that silence was wisdom, that holding back was harmless, that someone else (someone more qualified) would step in eventually.

But deep down, I knew the truth: I wasn't protecting the moment. I was abandoning it.

Maybe you've been there too. The opportunity was right in front of you. You felt the nudge. Your heart was racing. You knew God opened the door, but silence felt safer. The words never made it past your lips.

And afterward, you replayed the moment, wishing you could go back. Wishing you had said something.

Here's the tension we must face:

Every time we stay silent, the enemy celebrates. Every time we choose comfort over courage, we miss a moment God wanted to use.

But what if it didn't have to be that way anymore?

What if fear wasn't the loudest voice in your life?

What if you learned to recognize those God-moments and step into them with confidence?

The truth is, most Christians know this tension. Research shows that only 45% of churchgoers say they've shared how to become a Christian with someone in the past six months.

That means more than half of us are silent about the very news that changed our lives. Why? Because fear, insecurity, and excuses have muted us.

But here's the antithesis of Silent Christianity:

"Faith comes by hearing" (Romans 10:17, NIV).

If the gospel isn't spoken, it isn't heard. And if it isn't heard, people remain lost.

Right now, over 3 billion people (40% of the world) are considered unreached. That's not just a statistic. That's billions of eternal souls, many of whom will never set foot in a church building.

We can't keep waiting for pastors or pulpits to do the job. In a culture where fewer people attend church, the mission field has shifted. Evangelism must leave the stage and enter everyday life.

The early church understood this, and Jesus prepared us for it:

> *"But you will receive power when the Holy Spirit comes on you;*
> *and you will be my witnesses..."* ***(Acts 1:8)***

That promise still stands. The Spirit still empowers. And the Church still carries the responsibility to speak up.

As Shane Pruitt says, *"The lost aren't commanded to go to a church building—the Church is commanded to leave the building to go to the lost."*

Why This Book Exists

This book exists because silence has gone on long enough.

It's written for the believer who feels the weight of missed opportunities.

For the Christian who knows their faith has been on mute and longs to turn up the volume.

For the everyday disciple who wants to *live loud*, unashamed and obedient.

Across four sections, we'll tackle the problem head-on:

- **Why** we must break the silence
- **What** is causing our silence
- **Where** to start, beginning with the right theology
- **How** to begin living louder today

Read Slow. Act Fast.

This can't just be another book you finish and forget.

The goal isn't for you to admire a few good quotes; it's for you to look deeply into the truth of God's Word, and then honestly at your own life beside it. That's where change begins. That's where an evangelistic lifestyle is born, when reflection turns into action.

For once, let a book move you to do something that matters for eternity.

If you finish these pages, slide this book onto a shelf, and never step past your comfort zone to share the gospel, then these words will have been wasted.

But if you finish and find yourself stirred to live differently, to speak up, to see souls the way God does, to help your friends, coworkers, and family find Jesus—then every late night I spent writing will have been worth it.

We all need reminders, simple truths that wake us up to what's been right in front of us all along. It's like sitting in a dirty car every day and forgetting how messy it's gotten until someone says, *"Hey, it's time to clean this up."*

Maybe that's what this book is for you: a reminder to clean up the apathy and laziness that's crept into your faith and to care again about what really matters: eternity.

A New Lens

From this day forward, put on new spiritual lenses.

See people as God sees them, as eternal souls who matter. When you are in Christ, your perspective changes. Paul said in 2 Corinthians 5 that we no longer view anyone from a worldly point of view.

We see differently now.

We're living among the dead, surrounded by people blinded by the god of this world. But we've been given the mind of Christ and the ability to see with compassion, truth, and urgency.

So let me warn you one last time: this book isn't for the Christian who wants to stay comfortable. It's not for those who want to settle back into "everyday American Christianity."

It's for those willing to be stretched, to change—to risk obedience so that others might find hope.

You don't have to scream in Hobby Lobby at 99 decibels. But you do have to speak.

Because the gospel is the greatest news in the world, and it deserves to be heard.

SECTION ONE

THE WAKE-UP CALL

"Hell rejoices when the Church loses its voice."
– Leonard Ravenhill

CHAPTER 1:
THE VOLUME IS DOWN

"How, then, can they call on the one they have not believed in? And how can they believe in the one of whom they have not heard? And how can they hear without someone preaching to them?" -**Romans 10:14**

Have you ever noticed how unsettling silence in the car can be? At first, it doesn't seem like a big deal. Maybe you turned the music down after a call and forgot to bring it back up, or maybe you lowered the volume to hear the GPS voice saying, "Turn left in 300 feet," like she's running your life. But after a while, the quiet starts to feel uneasy.

At first, you think, *No problem—a little silence is good.* But then you begin to notice every sound: the hum of the engine, the squeak of the wipers, even that mysterious rattle you've been pretending doesn't exist. Soon, the quiet feels less like peace and more like that awkward pause in a conversation when you're just wishing someone would say something.

Almost without thinking, your hand reaches for the dial. It's instinctive; your brain says, *Quick, fill the silence with something.* Music, a podcast, a phone call; anything but nothing.

That instinct says a lot: we don't like silence. Yet many of us live our faith the same way: on mute. We coast. We go through the motions. We let the gospel fade into the background like a song we've stopped noticing.

But just as you'd never drive forever in silence, faith isn't meant to stay quiet. It's meant to be turned up: loud, bold, and unignorable.

When we realize our spiritual volume has dropped, it's not a reason for shame—it's a wake-up call. A reminder to shift gears, reach for the dial, and let our lives amplify the hope of Jesus. Because when we live quietly, the world misses its chance to hear the melody of truth. But when we live with urgency, the world hears the song of salvation loud and clear.

THE COMMAND THAT CANNOT BE IGNORED

That's why we must ask: Why should Christians share the gospel?

The answer is both simple and staggering, because Jesus told us to.

In *Mark 16*, the resurrected Christ appeared to His disciples. After three years of teaching, sacrifice, and miracles, this was His final moment with them before ascending to heaven. He could have said anything. He could have thanked them or comforted them.

Instead, He gave them a command that would ignite a global movement:

> *"Go into all the world and preach the gospel to all creation. Whoever believes and is baptized will be saved, but whoever does not believe will be condemned."* (**Mark 16:15–16**)

Don't rush past that. This isn't a casual suggestion; it's where conviction meets calling. These are the final words of the King of kings, giving His followers their marching orders.

Imagine being there. After three years of walking beside Jesus, you're gathered for one last conversation. The weight of His words would linger in the air. This wasn't a soft encouragement to *do your best*. It was a clear command: continue what I started.

His commission was simple: evangelize. The Great Commission wasn't given to the most talented, confident, or outspoken; it was given to every believer who has experienced the power of the gospel.

Sharing Jesus isn't just something we do; it's part of who we are. The moment we were rescued, we were also recruited. Evangelism isn't optional; it's evidence. It proves that our hearts have been transformed by the message we share.

And it ties back to the very beginning, when He first called His disciples:

"Follow Me, and I will make you fishers of men."
(Matthew 4:19, ESV)

His first words matched His final words. If we're not fishing, we're not following.

OBEDIENCE FLOWS FROM LOVE

Sharing our faith isn't just about obedience; it's about love. Jesus said,

"If you love Me, keep My commands." **(John 14:15)**

Evangelism isn't about checking a box or meeting a quota; it's an overflow of love that comes from our relationship with Him.

I've learned this firsthand in marriage. When my wife, Bailee, asks me to do the dishes or change our son's diaper, I don't jump up because I'm afraid of her wrath (though, let's be honest—hangry Bailee is a force to be reckoned with). I do it because I love her. Love moves me to action.

When love leads, the "chore" stops feeling like a chore. Washing dishes becomes an act of service. Changing a diaper becomes a way of caring. Even running to the store for the millionth time that week turns into an expression of, *"I'm here for you, and I love you enough to do this."*

It's the same with Jesus. Sharing our faith isn't about duty—it's about devotion. It's not guilt-driven; it's love-driven. Just as I don't want my marriage to become a list of "husband chores," Jesus doesn't want our walk with Him to feel like a lifeless checklist. He wants obedience that flows from love.

When love is the fuel, evangelism stops being a burden and starts becoming a joy. We share because we *want* to, not just because we *have* to. Silence isn't only disobedience; it's unloving.

SIMON SAYS VS. JESUS SAYS

When I teach students, I love illustrating this truth with a simple game: Simon Says.

If you've played, you know the rules—you only obey when the command begins with *"Simon says."*

So I'll start a round by saying, "Everybody, stand up." Without fail, half the room pops up like popcorn. The other half? They realize too late that they've already lost. Then I'll say, "Simon says clap," and suddenly I've got an entire room applauding while I bow like they're giving me a standing ovation. It always gets laughs. Sometimes I'll even throw in a goofy command just to test their limits: *"Simon says hop on one foot,"* or *"Simon says pat your neighbor's head."*

And they do it, laughing the whole time, because the rule of the game is simple: when Simon says, you obey.

Then I drop the challenge: Why is it that when Simon says "stand up" we stand—but when Jesus says "speak up," we sit in silence?

It's sobering when you think about it. We'll follow the voice of a pretend leader just to avoid losing. We'll obey silly commands just to stay in the game. Yet the voice of the Son of God, the One who gave His life for us, calls us to love our neighbor, share the gospel, and make disciples... and we freeze. We laugh and move quickly when Simon speaks, but hesitate and make excuses when Jesus does.

Here's the truth: Simon didn't die for us. Jesus did.

He isn't just Savior, He is Savior *and* Lord. And His command to proclaim the gospel isn't optional; it's essential. We weren't saved to sit in silence; we were saved to be sent.

And here's the deeper truth: obedience in *Simon Says* lasts a few minutes and earns a laugh or bragging rights.

Obedience to Jesus?

It changes eternity.

This isn't a one-off command. The entire New Testament beats with the same drum of living loud:

"We are therefore Christ's ambassadors, as though God were making his appeal through us. We implore you on Christ's behalf: Be reconciled to God." **(2 Corinthians 5:20)**

"The fruit of the righteous is a tree of life, and whoever captures souls is wise." **(Proverbs 11:30)**

> *"To the weak I became weak, to win the weak. I have become all things to all people so that by all possible means I might save some." (1 Corinthians 9:22)*

Each verse points to the same truth: evangelism is not for the few, but for all. It's the normal Christian life.

A COMMAND THAT COSTS

Following Jesus was never meant to be convenient.

Evangelism isn't a hobby or a weekend getaway. It's obedience to a command that costs something. The gospel came to us through blood, sweat, and surrender, not comfort and convenience. When Jesus said, *"Go and make disciples,"* He wasn't inviting us into a safe mission. He was inviting us into a sacrificial one.

Obedience always requires courage. It may cost your reputation, your comfort, or your sense of control, but it always leads to life. Because the moment you start living boldly for Christ, the world will notice... and sometimes resist.

But that's okay.

After all, if your version of Christianity never costs you anything, it's not the version that came from a cross.

COUNTING THE COST

Every believer eventually faces a moment when obedience collides with comfort. It's that whisper from the Holy Spirit to speak when silence feels safer. It's that gentle nudge to love someone difficult, to give when it stretches you, or to stand for truth when it's unpopular.

That's where faith becomes real, not just something we believe, but something we live. Jesus never promised an easy road, but He did promise His presence on it.

When obedience feels heavy, remember this: the cross you carry is far lighter than the one He bore. And every time you choose to obey, even when it costs you, you're showing that your faith isn't quiet; it's alive.

GOD'S PLAN A

Here's the thing: God could have chosen any method to spread the gospel. He could have written it across the sky or sent angels to preach. But He didn't. He chose us.

That means you aren't Plan B. You aren't the backup option. You are Plan A.

So why break the silence? Because God Himself has commanded it. Because His perfect plan has placed both the responsibility *and* the privilege in our hands.

The next time you feel your faith growing quiet, remember this: just like you reach for the dial to turn up the music in your car, reach for the dial of your life. Turn it up. *Live loud.* Share boldly.

The world doesn't need quiet Christians. The world needs the volume of the gospel turned up, loud and clear.

REFLECTION QUESTIONS

1. When you think about the "volume" of your faith, is it loud and bold or quiet and muted? Why?

2. What emotions rise in you when you read Mark 16:15–16 as Jesus' final words to His disciples?

3. Why do you think so many Christians treat Jesus' commands as optional, like in the *Simon Says* game?

4. What does it mean for you personally to be God's Plan A for spreading the gospel?

ACTION STEPS

- Write down the name of one person in your life who needs Jesus. Commit to praying for them daily this week.

- Re-read Mark 16:15–16 and underline the verbs. Notice the urgency in "go" and "proclaim."

- Identify one area where you've been silent about your faith (work, school, social media). Ask God for courage to *turn up the volume.*

- Share your testimony in at least one conversation this week, even briefly. Treat it as practice for obedience.

> *"The church exists by mission, just as fire exists by burning."*
> **– Emil Brunner**

CHAPTER 2:
THE CONVERSATION THAT CHANGED A CITY

"For the Son of Man came to seek and to save the lost."
– Luke 19:10

It began as just another Saturday afternoon. My friend and I were strolling through Legacy West—a place alive with energy. Families laughed outside restaurants, music drifted from speakers, and shoppers moved in and out of stores like a steady current of motion and color.

That's when we met her.

Breanna.

At first glance, she seemed like any other young woman in her twenties, just enjoying the day. But then we asked the simplest question, "How are you?"

Her response caught us off guard. Tears welled up in her eyes, and she whispered, "My boyfriend and I just broke up."

Think about that. Out of all the polite answers she could've given, "I'm good," "Just fine," "Hanging in there", she chose the truth. Unfiltered. Vulnerable. Honest. With two strangers.

And in that moment, something became clear: people are desperate for hope. Sometimes, it takes only one small question to open a door to something far greater.

The crowd around us kept moving, but the world seemed to pause. I listened. I empathized. Deep down, I knew this encounter wasn't random; it was a divine interruption.

I leaned in.

I talked about the reality of brokenness and sin, but also about the God who sent His Son to make us whole again. I didn't speak in religious jargon; I simply shared what Jesus had done in my own life. Then I asked gently, "Have you ever experienced the love of Christ personally?"

Her answer was quiet but clear: "No."

And right there, outside a busy store, surrounded by noise and strangers, she bowed her head, tears streaming down her face, and prayed to receive Jesus.

In just twenty minutes, her story changed.

A breakup became a breakthrough.

Her bad news collided with the Good News.

I share this moment not to paint myself as a fearless evangelist (I've had my share of hesitant moments too), but to remind you: opportunities surround us every day. The harvest truly is plentiful. Our world is full of brokenness—and transformation will come only when followers of Christ choose to live as everyday evangelists.

JESUS' MISSION, OUR MISSION

Jesus Himself defined His mission in **Luke 19:10**: *"For the Son of Man came to seek and to save the lost."* Evangelism isn't optional for the Christian; it's central to who we are. To follow Jesus is to follow His mission.

John 4 paints this truth vividly. Jesus, weary from travel, sat by Jacob's well in Samaria. That detail matters. Jews typically avoided Samaritans, viewing them as outsiders and half-breeds. Rabbis especially wouldn't be seen alone with a Samaritan woman. But Jesus isn't bound by prejudice or cultural barriers. He looked past ethnicity and reputation; He saw a soul in need of saving.

He began with a simple request: a drink of water. Yet through that ordinary moment, Jesus revealed an extraordinary truth: He alone could quench the thirst of her soul. The woman had sought fulfillment through one relationship after another, yet none had satisfied. Only Jesus could.

If you look closely at the story, you'll notice something profound: Jesus was the seventh man in her life. She had five husbands, and the man she was living with wasn't her husband. Then came Jesus, the seventh. In Scripture, the number seven often represents completion or divine perfection. It's as though her long, painful search for love and identity finally found its true conclusion when she met Christ at the well.

Until that encounter, every relationship had left her empty, restless, and thirsty for something more. But with Jesus, the longing ceased. Her emptiness was filled not by another imperfect relationship, but by the living water of grace and truth that only He offers. The message is timeless: no human relationship, accomplishment, or possession can make us whole. True completion is found only in Jesus, the One who satisfies the deepest thirst of the human soul.

Then comes one of the most powerful moments in the story: *she left her water jar.* That small detail carries deep meaning. The water jar wasn't just a container; it represented her daily struggles, her isolation, and the very purpose that brought her to the well. Drawing water was an ordinary, necessary, even burdensome task; yet it symbolized her routine cares and old pursuits, the things she depended on for survival.

But after encountering Jesus, everything changed. She left the jar behind—a quiet but powerful symbol of transformation. She came to the well thirsty for water, but she left thirsting for God. Her priorities shifted. What once consumed her attention faded in the light of her new joy and purpose: to share Christ with others.

Transformed by that encounter, she ran back to her village, leaving her water jar at the well. That act spoke volumes. She was leaving behind her shame, her old life, and her misplaced hopes. Her heart now burned with one desire: to proclaim, *"Come, see a man who told me everything I ever did. Could this be the Christ?"* **(John 4:29).**

When Jesus truly fills a life, everything changes. The desire to please Him surpasses every other goal, and what once defined us no longer holds us. We, like the Samaritan woman, become living testimonies, carriers of the Good News to a world still thirsting for the Living Water.

Impacted people invite people. When a life is truly transformed, it naturally draws others in. The Samaritan woman's story proves this truth. Her simple testimony sparked curiosity, and Scripture records: *"Many Samaritans from that town believed in Him because of the woman's testimony"* **(John 4:39).**

Notice something remarkable: she hadn't gone through any evangelism training. She wasn't polished or rehearsed. She didn't have all the answers. She just shared what Jesus had done for her. And that was enough.

Her honesty carried power. Her transformation carried weight. Because of one woman's encounter with Jesus, an entire town experienced the ripple effect of grace. That's what happens when we allow Christ to change us from the inside out—our story becomes an invitation for others to meet Him too.

LIVING THE MISSION

Jesus interrupted her day, and her life was never the same. We are called to do the same—to intentionally interrupt people's lives with the gospel.

I was reminded of this truth one day while leading a group of students in street evangelism. Our team looked like a nervous SWAT squad, armed not with walkie-talkies but with gospel tracts, and definitely lacking in stealth. That's when I noticed a man completely engrossed in a book on a park bench.

My first instinct? *Don't bother him.* He looked deep in concentration, the kind of reader who might actually bite if you dared interrupt a good plot twist.

But then I remembered John 4, how Jesus interrupted the Samaritan woman's ordinary day at the well, and how that moment changed everything. So, taking a deep breath and whispering a quick prayer not to get scolded, I walked over, trying to appear as harmless as possible.

I asked what he was reading, silently hoping it wasn't a 900-page crime thriller about annoying strangers.

He looked up, slightly surprised—but to my relief, he smiled. We started talking, and before long, the conversation turned naturally toward faith.

That's when a bystander, let's call her *Captain Interrupt*, decided it was her personal mission to shut us down. She dramatically announced, "Stop bothering him!" loud enough for half the park to hear.

I braced myself, expecting the man on the bench to agree and tell me to leave. But instead, he spoke up calmly, still smiling. "They're not bothering me," he said. In fact, he added, our conversation was more interesting than his book.

In that moment, I almost hugged him, though I wisely restrained myself.

We talked freely and shared the hope of Christ, and I realized something again: most people aren't as annoyed by a spiritual conversation as we often think. Sometimes, God is simply looking for someone willing to interrupt, and willing to be interrupted. That day, a gospel seed was planted, not only in the man on the bench, but maybe even in *Captain Interrupt*, too.

Another time, the mission field found me in one of the most ordinary places imaginable, Walmart. I had pulled in for a grocery pickup (quite possibly one of the greatest inventions ever made). As I waited, a young man in football shorts came over to load the bags into my trunk.

We made small talk about school, practice, and of course, Friday night lights. His eyes came alive as he talked about his dream, playing college football, maybe even going pro. You could tell this wasn't just a hobby; it was his identity, his world.

Then, as he balanced a few remaining bags in his hands, I asked gently, "Let me ask you something. If football were taken away, if you couldn't play another down—would your life feel meaningless?"

He hesitated, then lowered his voice. "Honestly... yes. I don't know who I'd be."

Right there in that Walmart parking lot, with carts clattering by and the world rushing around us, his honesty opened a sacred moment. I shared how life is about more than success, performance, or what we do on the field, that there's a God who gives lasting identity, purpose, and meaning beyond any achievement.

Encounters like these keep me going. They remind me that the mission isn't complicated or reserved for preachers or professionals. The gospel transforms lives—and our part is simply to carry it everywhere: into everyday moments, grocery runs, conversations, careers, classrooms, neighborhoods, and yes, even sweaty locker rooms.

Every place can become a pulpit. Every heart is hungry for the hope only Jesus can offer.

WHEN WE LIVE LOUD

Living on mission isn't driven by selfish ambition or a desire for recognition. It's a daily choice to put others first, just as Jesus did. To live on mission is to live selflessly; to live for self is to miss the mission entirely.

When we embrace our identity as Christ's ambassadors, we become carriers of a hope far greater than ourselves, inviting others to experience the same joy and freedom we've found in Him. Scripture reminds us how much this matters: *"There is rejoicing in the presence of the angels of God over one sinner who repents"* (Luke 15:10). What could be more significant than partnering in the joy of heaven?

The story of the woman at the well shows that evangelism isn't about having all the answers, a spotless past, or a theology degree. It's about letting Jesus change you—and then letting that change speak. God used a Samaritan woman, an unlikely evangelist with a messy story, to invite her entire village to meet the Savior. The only true qualification for sharing the gospel is transformation.

If Jesus has changed the direction of your life, then your story carries power too. Don't hold back. Don't shrink away.

Live your faith out loud.

Share your testimony in everyday conversations.

Carry it into unexpected places.

Let it overflow with love and authenticity.

Because when you *live loud* for Jesus, heaven gets loud in celebration right alongside you.

REFLECTION QUESTIONS

1. When was the last time you experienced a divine interruption that opened the door to share Jesus? How did you respond?

2. What "water jars" might you need to lay down—those routines, comforts, or distractions that keep you from living on mission?

3. Which barriers (fear, busyness, discomfort, cultural pressure) hold you back from initiating gospel conversations?

4. How does the Samaritan woman's boldness inspire or challenge the way you share your faith?

_____

_____

_____

_____

ACTION STEPS

- Pray daily this week for one opportunity to "interrupt" someone with the gospel.

- Identify your mission field (your school, workplace, gym, or neighborhood) and begin one faith-filled conversation there.

- Share your story like the Samaritan woman: simple, honest, and centered on Jesus.

- Lay down your water jar by releasing distractions or excuses that keep you from living boldly and purposefully for Christ.

SECTION
TWO

WHAT'S SILENCING OUR SOULS

"*Obstacles are those frightful things you see when you take your eyes off your goal.*"
– Henry Ford

CHAPTER 3:
THE QUIET TRAP

> *"Therefore, since we are surrounded by so great a cloud of witnesses, let us also lay aside every weight, and sin which clings so closely, and let us run with endurance the race that is set before us."– Hebrews 12:1*

Growing up with a twin brother was both a blessing and a challenge; like having a built-in best friend and competitor rolled into one. We had a talent for driving our mom crazy, especially during long drives in her old three-seater truck. To survive those car rides, she'd pull out the classic *Quiet Game.* The rules were simple: whoever stayed silent the longest won.

As twins, we loved it—not because we enjoyed silence, but because it was another way to prove who was better. That's the thing about identical twins; you're born competitive when you live with your mirror image.

But today, many Christians are playing a very different kind of quiet game. It's not silence in the back seat; it's silence in the world. Culture tells us, *"Keep your faith to yourself. Nobody wants to hear about religion."* And far too often, we listen. We hold back, afraid that speaking up about Jesus might cost us friendships, opportunities, or reputation.

But think about this. My wife and I are currently expecting our second child as I write this. Can you imagine us going through all nine months of pregnancy without telling a single soul? That would be absurd! Imagine having such incredible news and choosing to keep it a secret.

Yet that's exactly what many believers do with the best news in the world: the cure for sin and the gift of eternal life. When we stay silent, we withhold hope. That's not humility, it's selfishness.

We hold the remedy for the deadliest disease known to humanity, yet too often we keep it bottled up. Why? We run into roadblocks, fears, lies, and distractions that mute our evangelism.

In this chapter, we'll uncover those roadblocks, face them honestly, and learn how to overcome them with courage and conviction, so we can speak boldly and live unashamed for the One who gave everything for us.

ROADBLOCK 1: LACK OF FAITH

Many Christians hesitate to share the gospel because they doubt that God can use them. They focus on their flaws and convince themselves they don't have what it takes. But Scripture reminds us that if you belong to Jesus, His Spirit already lives and works within you, empowering, guiding, and speaking through you. God doesn't wait for perfection before using someone. His Word has the power to ignite faith in others, even when yours feels small.

We often think, *"My faith isn't strong enough to share yet."* But the truth is, sharing our faith strengthens it. Evangelism isn't the reward for spiritual maturity; it's one of the ways we grow into it. As **Romans 10:17** declares, *"Faith comes by hearing, and hearing by the word of Christ."* Every time we speak about Him, our trust deepens too.

Consider the friends in Mark 2 who lowered the paralyzed man through the roof to reach Jesus. They faced barriers, but their faith found a way. It wasn't their eloquence, strategy, or perfection that moved Jesus—it was their simple, determined trust.

The lesson is clear: trust God enough to act. Strengthen your faith not in isolation, but in motion. Each time you take a step of faith, each time you open your mouth to speak about Jesus, your courage grows stronger, and your confidence in Christ becomes more unshakable.

ROADBLOCK 2: "IT'S NOT MY RESPONSIBILITY"

It's easy to assume evangelism is for the professionals: the pastors, the missionaries, or the outgoing Christians who always seem to have the right words. But Jesus' command to "go and make disciples" wasn't given to a select few; it was given to every single follower.

Still need convincing? Take out your phone, flip it to selfie mode, and look at your reflection. That's who God expects to carry His message. Every time you look in the mirror, remember—you are a reflection of His kingdom, an ambassador for Christ.

We are children of God, and also missionaries for God.

When He rescued you from sin, He didn't just save you *from* something; He saved you *for* something, a life on mission. Charles Spurgeon once said, "Every Christian is either a missionary or an impostor." You may never stand behind a pulpit, but your life is a pulpit. You may never preach a sermon, but your actions are already preaching one.

So wherever you go, classroom, office, home, or coffee shop— remember: you are sent.

ROADBLOCK 3: "NEVER DONE IT; NEVER WILL"

For many, the idea of evangelism feels foreign or intimidating—so they never begin. If you've never shared your faith, it's easy to dismiss yourself as someone who "just isn't gifted for that." But past inactivity doesn't excuse present obedience.

Interestingly, it's often new believers, those fresh from their first encounter with grace, who become the most contagious witnesses. Their excitement is unfiltered, their words unpolished, yet their authenticity pierces hearts. Like the woman at the well, they can't keep quiet after meeting Jesus.

Spiritual maturity was never meant to make us quieter; it should make us bolder. Evangelism, much like learning to walk, grows easier with practice. If you've been following Jesus for years but haven't yet taken this step, now is the perfect time to start. Your story matters. And it's worth telling, no matter how many "first times" you've missed.

ROADBLOCK 4: APATHY

Sometimes believers aren't held back by fear, but by indifference. Life gets busy, routines feel comfortable, and the eternal destiny of those around us quietly fades into the background. Over time, our hearts can grow numb to the reality that people without Christ are heading toward a lost eternity. Apathy whispers, "It's not my concern."

But how can we stay unmoved when souls around us are slipping into eternity without hope? **James 4:17** confronts us plainly: *"So whoever knows the right thing to do and fails to do it, for him it is sin."*

The answer to apathy isn't guilt, it's love. Revival begins on our knees: "God, break my heart for what breaks Yours." Ask Him to replace indifference with compassion and to rekindle your passion for the lost. When His love fills your heart again, evangelism stops feeling like an obligation and starts flowing as a natural overflow of His presence within you.

ROADBLOCK 5: WRONG MINDSET

Cultural and personal misconceptions often silence bold witness before it ever begins. Many believers have absorbed ideas like these:

- "Evangelizing at work or school is wrong."

  Yet those are some of the most strategic mission fields we have—places where we spend most of our waking hours. Your mission field isn't somewhere far away; it's wherever God has already placed you.

- "People don't want to talk about spiritual things."

  In truth, everyone is searching for meaning. Brokenness is universal, and Scripture reminds us that God has placed eternity in the human heart (Ecclesiastes 3:11). Beneath the surface, most people are quietly wrestling with life's deepest questions.

- "I'll get to it eventually."

  But eternity doesn't wait. Today may be someone's only chance to hear the truth. The gospel is only good news if it reaches people in time. Delayed obedience can cost lives.

Wrong thinking leads to weak living. Replace lies with truth from God's Word, and remember: your mission begins wherever your feet are.

ROADBLOCK 6: NOT KNOWING LOST PEOPLE

Many Christians live in what could be called a "holy huddle"—safe, comfortable, and surrounded only by church friends. But Jesus wasn't like that. He was known as a *friend of sinners* because He intentionally sought out people who needed rescue.

Yes, Scripture cautions us not to be corrupted by bad company (1 Corinthians 15:33), but there's a difference between being influenced and being an influence. Mission requires proximity.

Think about your own circles: your family, workplace, gym, and neighborhood. Who among them needs the hope of the gospel? Don't let comfort or community become a barrier to your calling. The gospel travels best through genuine relationships, not isolation.

ROADBLOCK 7: HABITUAL SIN

Nothing short-circuits courage more than hidden sin. When we keep things in the dark, shame grows, confidence shrinks, and boldness disappears. Galatians 5:17 reminds us that the flesh and the Spirit are locked in a constant struggle.

But failure is never final. God invites us into authentic community, not for condemnation, but for healing. James 5:16 highlights the power of confession and prayer, where accountability loosens the enemy's grip and restores our voice to witness.

The cross has already settled sin's penalty. Now the Spirit empowers us to live in freedom and share that same hope with others. Sin doesn't have to silence you; Jesus has already broken its power.

MOVING FORWARD

My prayer is that as you read this chapter, you've identified some of the roadblocks that may have held you back.

Awareness is the first step, but it can't be the last. The next step is action.

Life is too short, and eternity is too real for faith to sit idle. As Pastor Brian Mills said, "Don't let Hell be bigger than Heaven because you didn't put in the work." So, go to work. Conquer these obstacles through deepening faith, rekindled passion, and courageous obedience. Surround yourself with believers who share your mission and link arms together for the cause of Christ.

Because here's the truth: the gospel was never meant to be played like the quiet game. It was meant to be proclaimed, demonstrated, and lived out boldly and joyfully for the glory of Jesus Christ.

REFLECTION QUESTIONS

1. Which of the seven roadblocks in this chapter feels most personal to you right now, and why?

2. Have you ever believed one of the lies of a wrong mindset (like "It's wrong to evangelize at school" or "People don't want to hear")? How has that shaped your confidence to share your faith?

3. What holds you back from building deeper relationships with non-believers? What intentional change could you make this month?

4. How does ongoing or hidden sin affect your courage and confidence in witnessing for Christ?

5. What would your faith and your daily life look like if you truly believed God wanted to use you to change someone's eternity?

ACTION STEPS

- Identify one specific roadblock from this chapter and pray daily this week for God's strength to overcome it.

- Take one bold, practical step; send a text, start a conversation, or invite someone to church. Don't wait for the "perfect" moment; act in obedience.

- Ask a trusted friend or mentor to hold you accountable to live and share your faith with honesty and courage.

- Journal your next evangelism opportunity. Afterwards, reflect on what went well, what challenged you, and how you sensed God working through you.

"

"Fear is the enemy of faith, and silence is the accomplice."
– Unknown

"

CHAPTER 4:
BREAKING THE SOUND BARRIER

"For God has not given us a spirit of fear, but one of power, love, and sound judgment."
– 2 Timothy 1:7

Fear.

It's one of Satan's favorite weapons; a tactic he uses to silence believers and keep us from stepping out in faith. Fear creeps into our hearts, stills our voices, and convinces us to play it safe. Florence Nightingale once said, "How very little can be done under the spirit of fear." She was right. Fear has sidelined more Christians than persecution ever has.

After years of reading, researching, surveying, and walking through my own experiences, I can confidently say this: fear is the number one reason Christians stay silent. And the believers who once held the greatest potential often become the quietest when fear takes root.

But here's the good news: fear doesn't have to win. In this chapter, we'll uncover some of the most common fears that hold us back and learn how to replace them with biblical truth and bold faith.

FEAR OF REJECTION

Nobody likes rejection; it stings. Our pride urges us to avoid it at all costs. Yet when you experience rejection for the sake of the gospel, you're in good company. Jesus was rejected. His disciples were rejected. Every bold follower of Christ eventually faces pushback.

I remember taking a group of students to a park in Meridian, Mississippi. It was a perfect day, families picnicking, kids running, people everywhere. We divided into small teams, each armed with gospel tracts and eager hearts.

When we regrouped later, I noticed some students looked discouraged. One said quietly, "The first person we talked to rejected us." You could feel the disappointment in the air.

But my heart leapt. I smiled and said, "Praise God! That means you're doing it right."

Here's why: we're not responsible for the response, we're responsible for the message. Rejection doesn't mean failure; it means faithfulness. They're not rejecting you; they're rejecting Jesus. Our task isn't to convict or convert; it's simply to convey.

FEAR OF MESSING UP

"What if I say it wrong?"

"What if I forget a verse?"

"What if I stumble?"

If those thoughts have ever run through your head, you're not alone. But here's the truth: God never asked you to be perfect in evangelism. He simply asked you to be obedient.

Jesus promised in **Luke 12:12** that *"the Holy Spirit will teach you in that very hour what you ought to say."* That means when you step out in faith, you're not speaking alone. The Spirit of God stands ready to guide your words and steady your heart.

Now, that doesn't mean we shouldn't prepare—it means our confidence isn't in our eloquence, but in His presence.

Preparation still matters. Take time to memorize one or two gospel-centered verses that help you share clearly and confidently, such as:

> "For God loved the world in this way: He gave His one and only Son, so that everyone who believes in Him will not perish but have eternal life."*(John 3:16–17)*

> "But God proves His own love for us in that while we were still sinners, Christ died for us." *(Romans 5:8)*

> "He made the One who did not know sin to be sin for us, so that in Him we might become the righteousness of God." *(2 Corinthians 5:21)*

You don't have to preach a three-point sermon. The Bible is full of one or two-sentence summaries of the gospel. Sometimes a single verse and your personal story are enough. And here's the secret: even if your words come out imperfectly, your sincerity speaks louder than flawless delivery.

THE FEAR OF THE UNKNOWN

The unknown paralyzes many believers. What if I don't know how they'll respond? What if it gets awkward? What if it doesn't go anywhere?

But Scripture gives us an anchor: *"And remember, I am with you always, to the end of the age"* **(Matthew 28:20).** Jesus never sends us into the unknown alone; He promises His presence. And as 2 Corinthians 5:7 reminds us, we walk by faith, not by sight.

That means even when you don't know what's ahead, you know Who walks beside you. And that's enough.

FEAR OF THE "WHAT IFS"

What if they're not ready? What if I can't answer their questions? What if I offend them?

Let's settle this: the gospel will offend. Paul called it "a stumbling block" to some and "foolishness" to others. Our job isn't to make it comfortable, but to make it clear.

You won't have all the answers, and that's okay. Honesty and humility open more hearts than a polished argument ever could. Readiness? That's God's work. You don't know who's ready—but He does. And He's already at work long before you speak.

REPLACING FEAR WITH THE RIGHT FEAR

The answer isn't pretending fear doesn't exist—it's replacing it with the fear of the Lord.

Paul put it this way: *"Therefore, knowing the fear of the Lord, we persuade others"* **(2 Corinthians 5:11)**. This fear isn't terror; it's reverence. Awe. A deep respect that overpowers the fear of people.

Remember: *"God has not given us a spirit of fear, but one of power, love, and sound judgment"* **(2 Timothy 1:7)**. When fear knocks, answer with prayer. *"Don't worry about anything, but in everything, through prayer and petition with thanksgiving, present your requests to God"* **(Philippians 4:6)**.

Name your fears. Write them out. Pray them out. Then trade them for what God offers—power, love, and a sound mind.

OVERCOMING FEAR

When the angel appeared to the women at the empty tomb, his first words weren't an explanation or a headline. He didn't open with excitement, shouting, *"Hey, good news—Jesus is back and better than ever!"*

Instead, his first words were simple and steady: *"Do not be afraid."*

Out of everything heaven could have said in that moment, that's what God chose. And that choice matters.

These women had just endured three of the darkest days of their lives. They had lost not only a friend, but the One they had left everything to follow. They had watched His betrayal unfold. They had witnessed His crucifixion. They had stood at a distance as hope itself was buried.

Imagine the grief, the anxiety, the exhaustion. Imagine the questions that filled their hearts: *Was it all real? Did we waste our lives? Where is God now?*

It's in the middle of that emotional storm that the angel speaks, not to their situation, but to their hearts: *"Do not be afraid."*

The Greek word used here is "phobeō," meaning "don't be frightened, don't be gripped by fear." It's the same word the angel used earlier in Matthew 1, when he appeared to Joseph in a dream and said, *"Joseph, son of David, do not fear to take Mary as your wife."*

And that connection is powerful.

If we didn't have the first angel commanding *phobeō*, we wouldn't have this one encouraging *phobeō*.

Joseph needed to replace fear with faith so that God's plan could move forward through him. These women needed to do the same, to let faith rise when fear wanted to win.

And so do we.

The angel's words weren't just for that morning outside the tomb; they're for us today.

Because fear still whispers.

Fear of the future.

Fear of rejection.

Fear of failure.

Fear of not being enough.

Fear of being judged.

Fear of not belonging.

But here's the difference: we stand on this side of the resurrection.

Jesus has already defeated the grave, which means fear doesn't get the final word anymore.

We can walk in faith instead of fear, because the tomb is empty.

And when you follow the risen Christ, fear loses its grip.

Whatever's been keeping you quiet, anxious, or hesitant; hear the angel's words again:

Do not fear.

The resurrection grants every believer full permission to *live loud*.

A STORY OF COURAGE OVER FEAR

One morning, a pastor friend of mine, Ryan, shared a story over breakfast that I'll never forget.

The day after preaching a sermon on evangelism, he decided to practice what he had just preached. With his wife and child, he headed to a local park. Holding his little one in his arms, he approached a man sitting alone and began a simple conversation. For about thirty minutes, Ryan shared the gospel as naturally as he could.

The next day, he turned on the news and froze. The local station was warning residents about a potential murderer on the loose. "Do not approach this man; he is possibly armed," the newscaster said. When Ryan looked up at the screen, his heart dropped.

"Sweetie," he called to his wife, "isn't that the guy I talked to yesterday?"

It was.

The man Ryan had shared the gospel with was wanted for murder.

That moment reminded me and Ryan, that the gospel truly has no boundaries. God led him to speak to a murderer. That's how wide God's love stretches. He wants *everyone* to believe and surrender to Him, the gossipers, the liars, and yes, even the murderers.

It also reminds us of something else: God's protection and provision.

That encounter could've gone horribly wrong. Imagine approaching someone who had just taken a life, someone who might still be in fear, guilt, or panic. Ryan could've been harmed, and his family, too. Yet, while Ryan was holding his child close, God was holding Ryan even closer.

At our darkest moments, God still finds ways to reach us with His truth. That's His provision, and it often flows through His children.

Think about that. Ryan unknowingly shared the gospel with a suspected murderer. Was it risky? Absolutely. But it was also divine. God's protection surrounded him, and His love spoke through him.

We don't know whether that man ever responded in faith. But we do know this: he heard the truth about Jesus. And even murderers matter to God. He still uses His people to reach them.

SOMEONE GREATER THAN FEAR

Don't let fear win.

Don't let rejection, failure, the unknown, or the "what ifs" keep you silent. Live so loud in your faith that the enemy trembles when you speak.

Because the real reason many of us don't share our faith isn't that we *can't*, it's that we're *afraid*. And the real reason we *must* share our faith is because Jesus is greater than our fear.

REFLECTION QUESTIONS

1. Which fear do you struggle with most—rejection, failure, the unknown, or the "what ifs"? Why?

2. How has fear silenced your witness in the past? Be specific.

3. What truths from Scripture give you the confidence to share your faith boldly, even when fear rises up?

4. How does Pastor Ryan's story challenge your perspective on risk, courage, and obedience?

5. What would it look like to replace your fear of people with a holy reverence for the Lord in your daily life?

ACTION STEPS

- Name your fear. Write it down this week, pray over it, and trade it for God's promise of *power, love, and a sound mind* (2 Timothy 1:7).

- Memorize a verse. Choose one (John 3:16, Romans 5:8, or 2 Corinthians 5:21) and use it the next time you share the gospel.

- Take one bold step. Intentionally start a gospel conversation, even if it feels messy or uncomfortable.

- Reflect afterward. Journal how it felt, what God did, and how you saw His hand at work in the moment.

"Evangelism is not a professional job for a few trained men, but instead the unrelenting responsibility of every person who belongs to the company of Jesus."
– D.T. Niles

CHAPTER 5:
THE MYTHS THAT MUTE US

> *"Now when they saw the boldness of Peter and John, and perceived that they were uneducated, common men, they were astonished. And they recognized that they had been with Jesus." – Acts 4:13*

Evangelism is intimidating. For many Christians, fear makes the idea of speaking up feel impossible. And when fear creeps in, we often trade it for something easier—misconceptions.

These false views act like weeds. They choke out boldness and allow believers to settle for a quiet, Sunday-only version of Christianity.

But here's the truth: lost people matter to God. Every human being is created in His image, knit together in their mother's womb, loved deeply, and valuable to their Creator.

If we really believe that, we can't afford to let lies about evangelism cloud our mission. Before we talk about what evangelism *is*, we must clear away what it *is not*.

MISCONCEPTION #1: INVITING PEOPLE TO CHURCH IS ENOUGH

I love my church. I love how our pastor preaches unapologetically and how God moves week after week. I've invited friends, coworkers, even my barber—and many have shown up.

But inviting someone to church is not the mission. It's good, but it's not the main thing.

Jesus never said, "Go into all the world and invite people to your church."

He said, *"Go into all the world and proclaim the gospel to all creation."*

The church can support the mission. But it cannot replace the mission.

MISCONCEPTION #2: MY ACTIONS ALONE WILL LEAD PEOPLE TO CHRIST

A common mistake many Christians make is placing their hope in *lifestyle evangelism.*

Simply put, they try to live in such a way that their lifestyle alone will show others that God is real—hoping people will respond by placing their faith in Him.

St. Francis of Assisi is often credited with saying, "Preach the Gospel at all times. Use words if necessary." Personally, I prefer my friend Greg Stier's revision: "Preach the Gospel. It's necessary—use words."

There are two sides to this.

Yes, people absolutely notice a difference when we follow Jesus. The Bible even teaches in **John 13:35**: *"By this all people will know that you are My disciples, if you have love for one another."*

It's often said, "We are the Bible the world is reading." Our lives are letters, New Testament stories written by God and read by men.

Our love is evidence, but it is not the message.

Several years ago, I called in an order to Pizza Hut for a stuffed-crust Meat Lover's pizza—one of the greatest decisions Pizza Hut ever made was letting customers order ahead.

After arriving, I walked up to the counter to pay and pick up my order. The lady behind the register told me it wasn't ready yet and asked me to have a seat and wait.

At that point, I couldn't help but wonder, *"Why even bother calling ahead?"*

While wrestling with my impatient thoughts and an empty stomach, I noticed an older man at the counter where I had just been. He was finishing his order, counting out bills, and searching for loose change so he wouldn't have to break another.

With nothing else to do but people-watch, I decided to help. I dashed to the counter, reached into my pockets for leftover change, and placed it on the countertop. "Here, take whatever you need," I insisted.

Startled by my eagerness, the man looked at me and said something I'll never forget:
"You must be a Christian."

I smiled and replied, "Yes, sir."

In that moment, I felt proud someone had seen a glimpse of Christ in me. But as the feeling faded, a sobering realization hit: he had seen the fruit of my faith, yet I hadn't shared the seed that could truly save. He witnessed kindness but walked away without hearing about my Savior.

It struck me, this man could have left just as lost as when he arrived, still waiting for someone bold enough to connect genuine love with the life-changing message of the gospel.

Living a godly life does matter. Our actions break barriers, spark curiosity, and pave the way for spiritual conversations. But **Romans 10:17** reminds us: *"Faith comes from hearing, and hearing through the word of Christ."*

If we want others to truly find hope, forgiveness, and purpose in Jesus, we can't just live kind—we have to speak up. Love sets the table, but only the Word can satisfy the heart's deepest hunger.

MISCONCEPTION #3: IF THEY DON'T GET SAVED, I FAILED

Many believers equate evangelistic success with immediate, visible results: a conversion on the spot, a sinner's prayer, or a powerful story to share. But this mindset is not only unbiblical; it places an unnecessary weight of guilt on those faithfully sharing Christ, as if they alone hold the power to save. Evangelism was never meant to be a performance with a scoreboard. It's an act of obedience in partnership with God.

So, what does true success in evangelism look like?

1. **When you speak up.**

   Every time you open your mouth for Jesus, you are victorious. Each conversation breaks the silence of fear and moves you beyond your comfort zone. Simply obeying God's prompting is a win, regardless of the outcome.

2. **When someone hears.**

   The moment the gospel enters a person's ears; a seed is sown. Romans 10:17 reminds us: *"Faith comes from hearing, and hearing through the word of Christ."* You may not witness the fruit immediately, but God's word never returns void.

3. **When you water.**

    You might be the one who encourages, answers a question, or helps remove a barrier. As Paul wrote, *"I planted, Apollos watered, but God gave the growth"* (1 Corinthians 3:6). Every gospel conversation is part of God's greater process—sometimes you prepare the soil, sometimes you add water, and sometimes you get to see the harvest.

4. **When lives change.**

    Of course, seeing someone fully embrace Christ is a gift to celebrate. But remember: the miracle of regeneration is God's work, not a credit to your technique, arguments, or persistence. It's His Spirit that brings dead hearts to life.

True evangelistic success is not counted in decisions; it is measured in obedience. When you faithfully deliver the message, you have already succeeded. Results belong to God. Your "yes" is enough, because whenever you speak, God moves, whether visibly in the moment or invisibly in a soul.

MISCONCEPTION #4: EVANGELISM IS ONLY FOR THE GIFTED

One of the biggest lies Christians believe is that evangelism is reserved for the "professionals." Maybe we picture a fiery preacher on a stage or that one bold friend who seems to effortlessly share the gospel with everyone they meet. And quietly, we think, *That's not me. I'm not gifted like that.*

Here's the truth: Scripture never presents evangelism as a rare spiritual gift. Yes, Ephesians 4:11–12 tells us God gave the church evangelists—but notice their purpose: *"to equip the saints for the work of ministry."* Evangelists aren't meant to do all the evangelism themselves; they are given to train the whole body to live on mission. Evangelism isn't just for a select few— it's a calling for all of us.

Look at the first disciples. None of them was a professional speaker. They weren't polished communicators or theologically trained leaders. They were fishermen, tax collectors, zealots. Acts 4:13 says people recognized Peter and John as "unschooled, ordinary men." And yet these ordinary men shook the Roman Empire, not because of perfect words or flashy skills, but because, as the text says, "they had been with Jesus."

That's the difference. Not gifting. Not titles. Not eloquence. The presence of Jesus.

You don't need a seminary degree or a dynamic personality to share the gospel. You don't need to wait for a special moment where you feel uniquely qualified. What you need is the Spirit of God dwelling in you, the truth of God's Word shaping you, and the courage to speak when God opens a door.

Evangelism isn't a performance for the talented—it's obedience for the faithful.

REMOVING THE LIES

For too long, we've believed the lie that silence is safe. That staying quiet somehow preserves our faith. But silence doesn't protect faith; it paralyzes it. Every time we choose comfort over calling, fear over faith, or apathy over action, we drift further from the mission we were made for. The world doesn't need a silent Church; it needs a faithful one.

That's why this next part matters.

Because somewhere along the way, we forgot that faith isn't meant to be quiet. We've grown accustomed to half-hearted Christianity that hides behind screens and excuses. But it's time for that to end.

WAKE UP THE WORLD

Many believers have traded boldness for comfort and conviction for convenience. We started whispering the name that was meant to be shouted. The enemy doesn't have to destroy your faith if he can dull your passion, and for too many of us, that's exactly what's happened. But the gospel was never meant to be quiet. You weren't saved to sit still. The same Spirit that raised Jesus from the dead didn't fill your lungs so you could stay silent. It's time to wake up, speak up, and live out the message that still changes lives.

You weren't made to invent a new religion called *Silent Christianity*.

God didn't save you to blend into the background. He sent you as a bold, noisy, Spirit-filled ambassador to represent His Kingdom in a world desperate for truth.

He could have chosen angels to carry His message. But He chose something more personal.

He chose you.

Be obedient. The clock is ticking. Heaven's alarm is set. The return of Christ is closer than it's ever been, and the world is still sleeping. Don't wait for the trumpet to sound. Rise now. Step out of spiritual slumber and reach people before they drift into eternal darkness.

Christianity isn't meant to be quiet. It's alive. It's active. It's real. And when we go silent, something inside us begins to die because silent Christianity is deadly Christianity.

TRUTHS TO REMEMBER

1. **God has already won.**

   Victory has already been declared. Jesus didn't come to try; He came and finished the fight. When He walked out of the tomb, He didn't just conquer death for Himself; He conquered it for you. Stop living like you're still losing. Every battle, setback, and struggle is already covered by the blood of the cross. When you walk in God's purpose, you don't fight for victory; you fight from it.

2. **You weren't made to be a background character.**

As the students say, "Don't be an NPC." God didn't write you into His story to stand in the background while others take action. You were created for a purpose that carries eternal weight. Life is too short and eternity too real to stay on autopilot, scrolling through moments instead of stepping into a mission. God's story is still being written—and He's looking for believers who will *live loud* enough to be part of it. Don't settle for being a spectator when God has called you to make a difference.

3. **There's no greater thrill than seeing God perform a miracle through you.**

Nothing compares to the moment you realize God just used you to change someone's eternity. Leading someone to Christ isn't just a conversation. It's heaven colliding with earth. Their eyes light up. Their heart awakens. You feel the Holy Spirit move, and in that moment, it all makes sense. This is why you were made. It's not pressure; it's privilege. There's no greater rush than being part of someone's rescue story.

4. **Your friendships could change forever if you share the gospel.**

Think about your closest friends, the ones you laugh with, hang out with, and share life with. What if the greatest thing you ever gave them wasn't a memory, but the message of eternal life? Sometimes we hesitate because we fear losing a friendship, but that very friendship could be the bridge God uses to reach them. The conversation you avoid today might become the story they tell for the rest of their lives: "It was my friend who told me about Jesus." That's not awkward. It's actually beautiful.

5. **Your family could experience freedom if you step out in faith.**

The people closest to you may be the hardest to talk to about faith—but they also need to see it most. Maybe the change you've been praying for isn't waiting on them; it's waiting on your obedience. When you lead with love and speak with truth, God can use your courage to unlock chains that have held your family for years. One bold conversation, one prayer, one act of obedience can spark revival.

6. **There is always a cost to following Jesus.**

The cross was never a symbol of comfort. It was a symbol of surrender. Following Jesus will always cost something: comfort, popularity, approval, or even relationships. But the cost of comfort is nothing compared to the reward of obedience. Every time you follow Him when it's inconvenient, you declare that your faith is real. Discipleship isn't cheap, but it's always worth it.

7. **Let the God of all comfort meet you outside your comfort zone.**

God never promised comfort; He promised His presence. Every time you take a step of faith that stretches you, He meets you there. When your hands shake and your voice trembles, He strengthens you. When fear whispers that you're not enough, He reminds you that He is. Faith doesn't silence fear. It moves forward anyway. The safest place in the world isn't your comfort zone. It's the will of God.

So *live loud*. Wake up the world before the alarm sounds.

REFLECTION QUESTIONS

1. Which misconception about evangelism have you believed in the past, and how has it affected your willingness to share the gospel?

2. Do you rely more on "lifestyle evangelism" than actually speaking the gospel? Why do you think using words feels difficult?

3. How do you currently define success in evangelism, and how does that compare with the biblical perspective in this chapter?

4. Do you see evangelism as a calling for all Christians, or something only for the "gifted"? How should this shift your mindset?

5. What misconceptions about evangelism do you notice most in your church or community?

ACTION STEPS

- Identify one misconception from this chapter that has held you back, and pray this week for God to replace it with truth.

- Start one gospel conversation this week—don't just invite someone to church or show kindness; use words to point clearly to Jesus.

- Redefine success in evangelism. Write a new definition based on obedience, not outcomes, and keep it in your Bible as a reminder.

- Encourage someone else. Share the truths from this chapter with a friend, reminding them that evangelism is not just for the "gifted," but for every believer.

SECTION
THREE

THE POWER BEHIND THE VOLUME

"
"Imagine having the greatest message in the world—and no one willing to deliver it."
-Unknown
"

CHAPTER 6:
THE MESSAGE THAT MATTERS MOST

"For I am not ashamed of the gospel, because it is the power of God for salvation to everyone who believes." – **Romans 1:16**

As a student pastor, one of my favorite moments is watching students step out of their comfort zones to share their faith. I'll never forget a day at the mall when we set out to evangelize. If you've never done this before, it's not about shouting at people or cornering them with signs—it's about simple, genuine conversations.

Inside a Foot Locker, I spotted two teenage boys checking out Jordans. With a nudge from the Spirit, I motioned to our group, and together we walked in. At first, it was all small talk—favorite shoes, styles, sports. Then came the shift.

"Have you guys ever heard of the greatest news ever to exist?" I asked.

"No," they replied.

That's when I leaned in: "We're actually going around sharing it with people. Would you want to know this good news?"

They shook their heads. So right there, surrounded by sneakers, we walked through the gospel, clear, simple, from A to Z. And the best part? It wasn't just me. The students I brought along joined in, sharing pieces of truth, filling in details, and encouraging the boys. It was a team effort.

As we wrapped up, I asked, "Dylan and Crue, would you like to trust in Jesus to forgive you of your sins right now?" One of them slowly put the Jordans back on the shelf. Then, in the middle of Foot Locker, we bowed our heads. Those teenage boys cried out to God for forgiveness.

That moment reminded me: the content of our message matters. And when delivered with clarity, courage, and community, the gospel still changes lives.

THE GOSPEL IN FOUR MOVEMENTS

Over the years, I've discovered that the gospel isn't just a story to be told, it's a message that changes everything. Yet sometimes we overcomplicate what was meant to be simple. James Merritt summarizes the gospel in a way that is both clear and systematic: the Bad News, the Worst News, the Good News, and the Best News.

It's more than a catchy outline; it's a roadmap through the entire story of Scripture, from our fall to our redemption. Let's walk through it together.

1. THE BAD NEWS: WE HAVE ALL SINNED

Before we can appreciate the good news, we must understand the bad news. The Bible doesn't flatter humanity; it diagnoses us. We aren't "basically good people who occasionally mess up." We are sinners who have rebelled against a holy God. Sin isn't just breaking rules; it's breaking a relationship. It's cosmic treason against the Creator who made us in His image and for His glory.

> *"For all have sinned and fall short of the glory of God."*
> **(Romans 3:23)**
>
> *"None is righteous, no, not one."* **(Romans 3:10)**

Think of it this way: if perfection is the standard, even our best efforts miss the mark. The Greek word for "sin" (*hamartia*) literally means "to miss the target." Whether through pride, lust, greed, selfishness, or unbelief, every one of us has fired arrows that fall short of God's holiness.

Sin isn't just something we do; it's something we are. It's woven into our nature from birth (Psalm 51:5). That's the bad news: we are separated from the very God who made us to know Him.

2. THE WORST NEWS: WE CAN'T SAVE OURSELVES

If sin were merely a bad habit, we could fix it. But sin is a spiritual death sentence, and no amount of moral effort can revive a dead soul.

> *"For the wages of sin is death."* **(Romans 6:23a)**
>
> *"Your iniquities have separated you from your God."*
> **(Isaiah 59:2)**

We often try to bridge the gap to God through religion, charity, or "being a good person." But imagine trying to jump across the Grand Canyon. Some might jump farther than others—but no one makes it across. That's the human condition:

some may appear more moral than others, but everyone falls short of perfection.

This is the worst news: not only have we sinned, but we are powerless to fix it. Humanity's greatest problem isn't a lack of education, money, or morality; it's a lack of righteousness. No self-improvement plan can revive a dead heart.

Let that sink in. Let it keep you awake. Think about the people you know who are far from God. Don't stop at feeling burdened; do something. When your eyes are open to eternity, silence is no longer an option.

3. THE GOOD NEWS: GOD DID WHAT WE COULDN'T DO

Here's where grace interrupts the story. God didn't leave us hopeless. He didn't demand that we climb to Him; He came down to us. Out of unstoppable love, God sent His Son, Jesus Christ, to do what we could never do.

Jesus lived the sinless life we failed to live, died the death we deserved, and rose again to give us the life we could never earn. The cross is where God's justice and mercy collided—where sin was punished and sinners could be pardoned.

"But God proves His own love for us in that while we were still sinners, Christ died for us." **(Romans 5:8)**

"Christ Jesus came into the world to save sinners." **(1 Timothy 1:15)**

"For God so loved the world that He gave His one and only Son, that whoever believes in Him shall not perish but have eternal life." **(John 3:16)**

Never share the gospel without the resurrection. The empty tomb is God's receipt—the proof that Jesus' sacrifice worked. Death has been defeated. New life is possible.

The cross shows His sacrifice.

The empty tomb shows His power.

Together, they show His love.

4. THE BEST NEWS: WE CAN BE FORGIVEN AND FREE

The gospel doesn't stop with what Christ did; it moves to what we can do in response. Forgiveness isn't automatic; it must be received. God offers salvation as a free gift, but like any gift, it must be accepted.

"If you confess with your mouth, 'Jesus is Lord,' and believe in your heart that God raised Him from the dead, you will be saved." **(Romans 10:9–10)**

"Everyone who calls on the name of the Lord will be saved." **(Romans 10:13)**

"For you are saved by grace through faith... it is God's gift—not from works, so that no one can boast." **(Ephesians 2:8–9)**

This is the best news: no one is beyond hope of experiencing forgiveness.

THE GOSPEL: NO ONE IS TOO FAR GONE

The same power that raised Jesus from the grave can raise you from spiritual death.

Salvation isn't about trying harder; it's about trusting deeper. It's not about achieving righteousness; it's about receiving grace. You can't earn it, buy it, or deserve it. You simply believe and receive.

And that's why evangelism is never complete without an invitation. The gospel always calls for a response. It's not just information to agree with; it's a decision to surrender to.

The Bad News shows our need.

The Worst News reveals our helplessness.

The Good News displays God's love.

The Best News invites our response.

That's the gospel.

THE GREATEST NEWS STILL WORKS

This is the message we carry into malls, schools, neighborhoods, workplaces, and homes. The greatest news isn't just a concept—it's a call to action. It's God's rescue mission, delivered through ordinary people like us.

Let me ask you: Who will you share this news with? What's keeping you from speaking up? The message hasn't changed. And neither has its power.

Something needs to change, because the world is still waiting to hear it.

REFLECTION QUESTIONS

1. When was the last time you saw the gospel clearly change someone's life? How did that moment impact you?

2. Which part of the four movements (Bad News, Worst News, Good News, Best News) is hardest for you to explain? Why?

3. Why do you think it's so important to include the resurrection whenever you share the gospel?

4. Who in your life needs to hear "the greatest news," and what's holding you back from telling them?

5. How does Romans 1:16 challenge your view of boldness in sharing your faith?

ACTION STEPS

- Practice clarity: Write out the gospel in your own words this week using the four movements.

- Memorize Scripture: Learn one verse from each of the four categories (Romans 3:23, Romans 6:23, Romans 5:8, Romans 10:9–10) so you're always ready.

- Start a conversation: Ask someone in your circle, *"Have you ever heard the greatest news in the world?"* and be ready to share.

- Journal your response: After sharing, record how it went, what you learned, and how you saw God at work.

"The gospel is not good advice to be obeyed, it is good news to be believed."
– J.I. Packer

CHAPTER 7:
WHEN HEAVEN FILLS YOUR LUNGS

"Pray also for me, that the message may be given to me when I open my mouth to make known with boldness the mystery of the gospel." – **Ephesians 6:19**

There's one ingredient missing from the church today. Confidence. Believers desperately need more confidence. Without it, silence takes over. With it, the gospel spreads like wildfire.

Think about it: how many people in your life haven't heard about Jesus because you lacked the confidence to bring Him up? If you're honest, the number might sting. I know it does for me. Missed opportunities stack up quickly when fear wins. But history (and Scripture) show us that when believers step out in confidence, God does extraordinary things.

I saw this firsthand with a preteen named Jorden. During one of our services, she placed her trust in Christ. A few days later, our staff called her parents to celebrate. That conversation turned into something unexpected.

Her mom explained that their family was Catholic. When Jorden got home that night, she told her parents about her decision and announced that she wanted to be baptized.

Her mom replied, *"That's nice, Jorden, but you've already been baptized."*

Jorden looked at her mom with childlike honesty and said, *"No, mom. This is different. I don't think you have a personal relationship with Jesus. We were told to interrupt people if they don't know Him. So... I'm sorry to interrupt you, but you need to find Jesus."*

Stunned, her mom said, *"What? I know Jesus."*

But Jorden pressed, *"Yeah, but do you have a relationship with Him?"*

That boldness floored her parents. Later, her mom admitted, *"We were so surprised by our daughter's confidence that we actually started talking about visiting your Baptist church."*

One student's courage opened the door for an entire family to consider the gospel. That's the power of confidence.

CONFIDENCE FROM THE SPIRIT

In *Acts 4*, Peter and John stood before the religious council, questioned for healing a disabled man. Scripture says:

> *"Then Peter, filled with the Holy Spirit, said to them, 'Rulers of the people and elders: if we are being examined today about a good deed done to a disabled man—by what means he was healed—let it be known to all of you and to all the people of Israel, that by the name of Jesus Christ of Nazareth, whom you crucified and whom God raised from the dead—by him this man is standing here before you healthy.'"* **(Acts 4:8–10)**

Peter's confidence didn't come from personality, training, or quick thinking. It came from the Spirit of God. In fact, Jesus had already promised this moment:

> "When they bring you before synagogues and rulers and authorities, don't worry about how you should defend yourselves or what to say. For the Holy Spirit will teach you at that very hour what must be said." *(Luke 12:11–12)*

The promise was fulfilled. And the same Spirit that filled Peter fills us today. Confidence within begins with the Spirit within.

ORDINARY PEOPLE, EXTRAORDINARY BOLDNESS

The religious council couldn't believe what they were seeing. Two fishermen—not scholars, not orators, not influencers. And yet, *Acts 4:13* records:

> "Now when they saw the boldness of Peter and John and perceived that they were uneducated, common men, they were astonished. And they recognized that they had been with Jesus."

Let that sink in. Two ordinary men, no formal training, no credentials, no social standing—stood fearlessly before the most intimidating leaders in their nation. Their secret wasn't eloquence or education. It was an encounter.

The Greek word for boldness here, *parrēsia*, conveys openness, unreserved speech, and courageous confidence. It's the same word Paul used when he said his goal was to *"honor Christ with full courage, whether by life or by death"* **(Philippians 1:20)**. It's the kind of courage that refuses to hide, the kind of confidence that comes from conviction, not comfort.

Somewhere along the way, the Church lost some of that *parrēsia*. We traded boldness for politeness, truth for tolerance, and passion for preference. We became cautious where the early believers were courageous. As one evangelist said, "Churches either evangelize or fossilize." The difference between Christianity that thrives and Christianity that fades is confidence, the kind that comes not from personality, but from proximity to Jesus.

Where does that confidence come from? Peter and John didn't find their courage on a stage or in a seminary; they found it in the presence of Christ. **Acts 4:13** says the leaders *"recognized that they had been with Jesus."* That's the hinge of the story. Their confidence wasn't rehearsed; it was reflected. They had spent time with Him, and you can't spend time with Jesus without becoming bold about Jesus.

A seminary professor once told his students, *"Those who spend time with Jesus can't help but spend time telling others about Jesus. And those you tell can tell whether you've been with Him."*

True confidence can't be manufactured; it's cultivated in a quiet place. It grows in prayer, deepens in Scripture, and overflows in conversation.

LEARNING FROM PHILIP

This same Spirit-born boldness shows up again in *Acts 8* with Philip and the Ethiopian eunuch. Philip had just experienced revival in Samaria—crowds listening, people being healed, the Spirit moving mightily. If it were us, we'd want to stay where the energy was. But God had other plans.

When the angel told Philip to leave the crowds for one man on a desert road, he didn't argue or ask for details. He simply obeyed. That alone is confidence, trusting that God's plan is better than your platform.

On that lonely stretch of desert, Philip met the Ethiopian eunuch, the treasurer of the queen, an influential, wealthy, educated man. By human standards, Philip had no reason to approach him. But filled with the Holy Spirit, he ran to the chariot (*Acts 8:30*) and began a conversation that would change eternity.

When the eunuch admitted he didn't understand the passage in Isaiah, Philip didn't hesitate. He climbed in, opened the Scriptures, and introduced him to the Savior. The result? One man was transformed, baptized, and sent home to Ethiopia carrying the gospel with him—possibly the first missionary to that region.

Philip's story gives us three powerful lessons for cultivating confidence.

1. STAND UP

When the angel said, *"Rise and go,"* Philip stood up. Confidence always begins with willingness.

God can't steer a parked car; you've got to move before He can direct. Too often, we wait for perfect conditions, the right mood, or ideal timing before obeying God's promptings. Spiritual confidence is born when you take the first step of faith, even when the next step isn't clear.

If you want to grow your confidence, start by simply saying *"yes"* to what God has already told you to do.

- Who in your life have you been avoiding a spiritual conversation with?

- What opportunity to serve, lead, or share your faith have you kept on pause?

- What if the only thing keeping you from confidence is your comfort zone?

Standing up might mean volunteering in church, inviting a friend to youth group, or praying publicly for someone at school. It's the act of saying, *"God, I'm available."* Confidence doesn't come from knowing every detail; it comes from knowing Who called you.

2. SEIZE OPPORTUNITIES

Next, the Spirit told Philip, *"Go over and join this chariot."* Without hesitation, Philip ran.

He didn't analyze, delay, or overthink. He recognized that the Holy Spirit was opening a door and decided to sprint through it.

That's what confident believers do—they see interruptions as invitations. Every day is filled with God-moments disguised as ordinary moments:

- The co-worker who seems discouraged.

- The classmate who starts talking about purpose or pain.

- The stranger at the coffee shop wearing a cross necklace.

Confidence is the courage to respond.

Try this: tomorrow, ask God in prayer,

"Lord, make me aware of who You're already working on around me."

Then pay attention. When you sense that nudge (the thought like *"text them"* or *"ask them how they're really doing"*) don't dismiss it. Move toward it.

Every step of faith strengthens your confidence muscle. The more you seize Spirit-led moments, the more you'll realize God was already there, waiting.

3. SPEAK UP

Acts 8:35 says, *"Then Philip opened his mouth."* Those five words describe every revival in history. God moves when His people open their mouths.

We talk easily about what we love—sports, food, music, relationships—but somehow freeze when it comes to faith. Confidence doesn't mean fear disappears; it means fear doesn't have the final say.

Courage doesn't always mean fear is absent. It's when obedience collides with fear, and truth wins.

When your heart pounds and your palms sweat, remind yourself: this message has eternal weight. The gospel you're sharing has the power to bring someone from death to life (*Romans 1:16*).

Practically, you can build this habit by:

- Sharing short pieces of your story, not full sermons.

- Memorizing one or two verses that summarize the gospel.

- Asking open questions like, *"Do you have a faith background?"*

- Praying before every conversation: *"Lord, speak through me, not just to me."*

Start small. Share your faith with a friend you trust. Talk about how Jesus has changed your life. Each time you do, you'll sense your confidence grow—because it's no longer about you; it's about Him.

UNLOCKING THE PRISON OF SILENCE

Confidence within isn't arrogance; it's assurance. It's not swagger; it's surrender. True confidence is the quiet fire of someone knowing who they are and whose they are. It's

Spirit-empowered courage that unlocks the prison of silence many believers live in. It's cultivated in time with Jesus, fueled by obedience, and tested in conversations that matter. Confidence doesn't eliminate fear; it simply obeys in spite of it.

When ordinary believers decide to stand up, seize opportunities, and speak up, the world takes notice—just like it did with Peter, John, and Philip. The church comes alive again, and the gospel moves forward with unstoppable force.

Here's the truth: God isn't looking for the most qualified; He's looking for the most available.

So stop waiting for the perfect moment.

Stop assuming boldness is only for "super-Christians."

Stop believing the lie that you need to have it all together first.

You already have everything you need, the Spirit of God living in you.

Spend time with Jesus. Listen for His prompting. And when the opportunity comes—stand, seize, and speak. Because the gospel doesn't need professionals, it needs people.

REFLECTION QUESTIONS

1. When you think about sharing your faith, what fears or insecurities hold you back the most?

2. How does Jorden's story of childlike boldness challenge your perspective on confidence in evangelism?

3. In Acts 4, the leaders recognized Peter and John had been with Jesus. Would people say the same about you? Why or why not?

4. Which of Philip's three actions—Stand Up, Seize Opportunities, Speak Up—do you most need to grow in right now?

5. How does spending time with Jesus build confidence for you personally?

ACTION STEPS

- Spend time in His presence. Commit to daily time with Jesus this week—Scripture and prayer specifically asking for boldness.

- Identify one opportunity. Ask God to open your eyes to one person today you can "seize" as Philip did.

- Open your mouth. Don't just be kind—actually speak the gospel to someone this week.

- Memorize Acts 4:13. Let it remind you that ordinary people with Jesus become bold witnesses.

"We must talk to God about men before we talk to men about God."
– E.M. Bounds

CHAPTER 8:
THE QUIET THAT CHANGES EVERYTHING

"The harvest is plentiful, but the laborers are few; therefore pray earnestly to the Lord of the harvest to send out laborers into his harvest." – **Matthew 9:37–38**

We've talked about why we share the gospel, how to prepare, and what practical steps can make evangelism part of everyday life. But before we rush into the "how," we must return to the Who.

Here's the truth: you can't save anyone.

You can plant seeds, tell stories, and extend invitations—but only God can open blind eyes and change hearts. The moment evangelism becomes about your ability instead of His authority, you've already lost sight of its source.

That's why every movement of God begins not with a microphone, but with a moment of prayer.

In Acts 4, before the believers preached again, they prayed again. They didn't ask for comfort or safety—they asked for boldness and power. The result?

> *"After they prayed, the place where they were meeting was shaken. And they were all filled with the Holy Spirit and spoke the word of God boldly."* **(Acts 4:31)**

The power came after the prayer.

Prayer is the ignition switch of evangelism. It's what turns conviction into compassion and effort into effectiveness.

Let's be honest: many of us try to do the work of God without the help of God. We brainstorm strategies, study methods, and perfect presentations—but forget to bow before the One who actually saves.

Research confirms what Scripture already teaches. According to Barna, less than 25 percent of Christians pray regularly for someone who doesn't know Christ. That means three out of four believers are trying to live on mission without ever talking to the God of the mission.

No wonder we're exhausted.

We've confused boldness with busyness. We've traded dependence for drive. We're trying to produce fruit without staying attached to the Vine (John 15:5).

That's the tension: God calls us to go, but He also calls us to pray. The most powerful evangelists in history have always been intercessors first.

- D.L. Moody once said, "Every great movement of God can be traced to a kneeling figure."

- Charles Spurgeon called prayer "the powerhouse of the church."

- Oswald Chambers wrote, "Prayer does not fit us for the greater work; prayer is the greater work."

If we truly believe that salvation belongs to the Lord (Psalm 3:8), then prayer is not optional—it's essential.

Jesus Himself emphasized this truth in **Matthew 9:37–38:**

"The harvest is plentiful, but the laborers are few; therefore, pray earnestly to the Lord of the harvest to send out laborers into his harvest."

Before He sent His disciples, He told them to pray. Why? Because evangelism isn't about persuasion, it's about God's Spirit convicting, saving, and converting.

THE POSTURE THAT PREPARES THE HEART

Prayer isn't the pre-game; it's the game. It's where the real work of evangelism begins.

When you pray for the lost, something shifts. You start seeing people not as interruptions, but as invitations. You begin noticing spiritual hunger behind casual conversations. Prayer softens your heart so you can carry God's heart.

There's power in bringing names before the throne of grace. When you tell someone, "I've been praying for you by name," it softens hearts and opens doors.

Mark Dever once said,

"Our continuing to pray for someone is a testimony of our faith; not in them or in ourselves, but in God."

Praying by name shapes conversations. Those names on your prayer list become names on your lips. Warren Haynes suggests following Jesus' pattern in John 17 as a framework:

- Pray for God's protection over them.

- Pray for God's provision in their life.

- Pray for a personal relationship with Christ.

Prayer also dismantles pride. It reminds us that we're not the Savior, we're the servant. We can't change hearts, but we can cry out to the One who can.

That's why prayerless evangelism so quickly becomes joyless evangelism. Without prayer, sharing your faith feels like a performance. With prayer, it feels like a partnership.

Prayer is a partnership with God's sovereignty. It shifts our reliance from clever words to His power. J.I. Packer described it this way:

"The prayer of a Christian is not an attempt to force God's hand, but a humble acknowledgment of helplessness and dependence."

True evangelism begins on our knees.

THE POWER THAT MOVES THE MISSION

Evangelism without prayer is like a car without gas; it may look ready, but it won't go anywhere.

Prayer fuels every mission. It turns conviction into compassion, fear into boldness, and opportunities into divine appointments. When you pray, you're not trying to get God to join your plan; you're aligning your life with His.

Paul understood this principle. Over and over, he asked the churches to pray for him—not just for safety, but for words and courage:

"Pray also for me, that whenever I speak, words may be given me so that I will fearlessly make known the mystery of the gospel." **(Ephesians 6:19)**

Paul didn't only pray for the saved, he prayed earnestly for the lost:

"Brothers, my heart's desire and prayer to God for them is that they may be saved." **(Romans 10:1)**

These are the kinds of prayers that shake kingdoms.

Imagine what could happen if believers everywhere prayed with that level of expectation. Picture homes, campuses, and workplaces where names are lifted daily before God—where intercession becomes as natural as breathing.

- What if every Christian prayed specifically and persistently for three lost friends?

- What if your church's prayer nights turned outward, asking for salvation instead of comfort?

- What if prayer became the spark that reignited your love for people far from God?

History proves it: revival never begins in a crowd—it begins in a closet.

Before you talk to people about God, talk to God about people. Every transformed heart begins in the unseen space of prayer. Greg Stier nails it when he says:

"We spend more time in announcements than in intercessory prayer, and we wonder why there's no revival."

LEARNING FROM JESUS' EXAMPLE

If anyone could have excused Himself from prayer, it was Jesus. He was the eternal Son of God in human flesh—performing miracles, healing the sick, casting out demons, teaching crowds, and discipling leaders. Yet despite possessing divine authority and supernatural power, Jesus still chose to pray.

Mark 1:35 captures the scene:

> "And rising very early in the morning, while it was still dark, he departed and went out to a desolate place, and there he prayed."

Notice the rhythm: *very early, still dark, desolate place.* Before the noise of the crowds. Before the demands of ministry. Before the disciples even opened their eyes, Jesus was already talking with His Father.

Prayer wasn't an accessory to His ministry; it was the engine that drove it. It wasn't a warm-up; it was the work. Every miracle, every sermon, every act of compassion flowed from the intimacy He cultivated in private.

If Jesus, the sinless Son of God needed daily time with the Father, how much more do we?

We live in a world that never stops buzzing. Notifications, responsibilities, and noise chase us from the moment we wake. That's why getting away to pray isn't just helpful—it's holy. It's not about escaping the world; it's about being equipped to re-enter it with the heart of Christ.

If you want to *live loud* for Jesus in public, you must learn to kneel low before Him in private. Boldness before people is always born from brokenness before God.

THE MISSING PIECE

Now imagine your next gospel conversation. You're ready. You've prepared. You start strong—smiling, listening, asking thoughtful questions. You quote Scripture with clarity. You walk through the gospel with precision. The person leans in. Every word lands perfectly.

And yet... nothing happens.

Their eyes stay glazed. Their hearts stay closed. The moment feels heavy, empty. Everything looked right, but something felt missing.

That missing piece? The power of God.

You can't manufacture that power. You can't rehearse it or fake it. It only comes through prayer. Prayer doesn't just prepare the moment; it fills the moment.

Before every gospel conversation you'll ever have, Jesus has already been praying for you. Scripture says He "lives to intercede" for us (Hebrews 7:25). Think about that: before you even open your mouth, He's already standing before the Father, interceding on your behalf.

Now it's your turn to join Him, to partner with His ongoing intercession through your own prayers.

That's why revival doesn't start with louder voices; it starts with lower knees. It's not fueled by confidence in your ability but by dependence on His Spirit.

When we pray before we proclaim, heaven partners with earth. When we depend on God's power instead of our own, the results are eternal.

Evangelism without prayer is powerless.

Evangelism with prayer is unstoppable.

Before you speak, stop and seek.

Before you go, kneel low.

Before you *live loud*, pray deep.

Because the loudest life you'll ever live for Christ begins quietly, with Him.

REFLECTION QUESTIONS

1. How often do you pray for people in your life who don't know Jesus by name?

2. Which area of prayer do you most neglect—personal time with God, intercession for others, or prayer with others?

3. How does knowing that Jesus Himself intercedes for you (Romans 8:34) change your perspective on evangelism?

4. In what ways has prayer softened your heart toward people who are difficult to love or reach?

5. What would your evangelism look like if prayer truly became the starting point for every conversation?

ACTION STEPS

- Pray Scripture. Use John 17 or Ephesians 1:15–23 as a framework to pray specifically for people's protection, provision, and salvation.

- Find a prayer partner. Commit to weekly prayer together for boldness and for lost people by name.

- Start your day in solitude. Follow Jesus' example (Mark 1:35) and spend early, quiet time with God before the noise of the day begins.

SECTION
FOUR

THE MOVEMENT STARTS HERE

"Evangelism without preparation is like a soldier going to battle without a weapon."
– Unknown

CHAPTER 9:
HOW TO BE READY WHEN GOD OPENS THE DOOR

> *"Always be prepared to give an answer to everyone who asks you to give the reason for the hope that you have. But do this with gentleness and respect."* – **1 Peter 3:15**

So far, we've uncovered the why of evangelism—why silence needs to be broken, what keeps us quiet, and what the gospel truly is. We've seen that evangelism isn't reserved for the elite few or the overly extroverted. It's not a personality trait; it's a posture of obedience.

By now, one truth should be clear: there's no magic formula, no secret hack. Evangelism isn't about perfectly worded speeches or memorized outlines. It's about the Spirit of God working through ordinary believers who are willing to *live loud* in a quiet world.

But here's the tension: willingness without preparation often turns into a missed opportunity.

We've all had those moments—doors open, conversations start, opportunities are right there, and yet fear, distraction, or uncertainty keeps us from stepping through. The Spirit prompts, but our lack of preparation paralyzes.

The Holy Spirit empowers us, but preparation equips us. The Spirit gives power, but discipline gives direction. When Spirit and strategy come together, confidence grows, and conversations multiply.

Think of it like an athlete training for a race. The race itself is unpredictable; weather changes, competition rises, but preparation builds endurance. In the same way, the believer who prepares doesn't just hope to share the gospel; they're ready to step in when God calls.

Evangelism isn't meant to be an afterthought. It's meant to become a rhythm; a way of life so ingrained in your routine that it becomes second nature. That's what this chapter is about: forming a new normal.

If the gospel really is the greatest news on earth, then it deserves the greatest intentionality in our lives.

WHY PREPARATION MATTERS

Jesus spent three years preparing His disciples before sending them out. They didn't just wake up one day and start preaching. He walked with them, taught them, challenged them, and equipped them. Preparation wasn't an obstacle to mission; it was the mission.

When the early church in Acts spread like wildfire, it wasn't by accident. They were filled with the Spirit and grounded in habits, meeting daily, praying constantly, and speaking boldly.

Preparation doesn't compete with faith; it fuels it. It doesn't replace dependence on God—it strengthens it.

We prepare because we believe God is going to move. And when He does, we want to be ready.

A NEW ROUTINE OF READINESS

In this chapter, I'm sharing practical tools and habits that have helped me, and countless others, step into evangelism with greater intentionality. Don't see these as boxes to check or rules to follow. See them as rhythms to build, habits that create margin, focus, and spiritual readiness.

Because preparation isn't about perfection, it's about posture. It's about building a lifestyle where evangelism is no longer an event you attend, but a way you live.

Imagine waking up every day with a sense of readiness, like a soldier trained for deployment, like an athlete stepping onto the field, like a believer stepping into a conversation that could change eternity.

That's the vision.

- A church full of prepared people is a church ready for revival.

- A believer who prepares is a believer God can use.

As you read through these next principles, don't just skim them, schedule them.

Don't just agree with them, apply them.

Don't just highlight them, habit-stack them into your daily life.

Because when preparation becomes routine, evangelism becomes reflex.

And when everyday believers live that way, the world won't just hear the gospel—they'll see it *lived loud*.

If passion fuels the mission, preparation drives it forward. These next tools aren't meant to complicate your faith; they're meant to clarify it. Think of them as anchors in your daily routine, habits that help you stay spiritually alert and mission-ready.

You don't need to do all of them overnight, but you can start somewhere today. Small, steady steps of preparation will shape you into the kind of believer who doesn't just wait for opportunities but walks into them.

Here are the practical rhythms that can turn your desire into discipline, your intentions into impact, and your faith into a lifestyle that lives loud.

1. MAKE A REACH LIST

Evangelism isn't about crowds, it's about faces. It's about people with names, stories, and eternal value. One of the most powerful tools you can develop is a Reach List, a simple list of people in your life who don't yet know Jesus.

Write them down. Don't keep them in your head; get them on paper. Neighbors. Coworkers. Classmates. Family members. Even the barista who remembers your latte order or the friend you see weekly at the gym.

Then pray for them by name. Ask God to open their hearts and open your eyes for opportunities to connect. Names keep things personal. As **Warren Haynes** said, "The most important word in any language is someone's name." When you write a name, you're writing a mission.

If your list feels short, that's a wake-up call. It might be time to step outside your Christian bubble. Go where people are: coffee shops, schools, sports fields, and workplaces. Jesus called fishermen, then told them to go fishing. Don't wait for opportunities, create them.

Next Step: Start a Reach List today with 3–5 names. Pray for them daily for one week. Watch how awareness shifts your heart.

2. MEMORIZE GOSPEL-CENTERED VERSES

When you share the gospel, you're not sharing your opinion—you're declaring God's truth. Scripture is sharper than any argument you could craft.

Memorizing gospel-centered verses gives you confidence when you speak and conviction when you doubt. They anchor your message in authority, not emotion. When your mind blanks, Scripture becomes your safety net.

Start with these foundational verses:

"For all have sinned and fallen short of the glory of God."
(Romans 3:23)

"For the wages of sin is death, but the free gift of God is eternal life in Christ Jesus our Lord." **(Romans 6:23)**

"For God so loved the world that He gave His one and only Son, that whoever believes in Him shall not perish but have eternal life." **(John 3:16)**

Imagine if every believer carried Scripture in their heart—speaking truth in hallways, classrooms, and offices. Even if Bibles were banned, the Word would still spread because it's hidden inside you.

Next Step: Pick one verse per week to memorize. Repeat it aloud daily until it becomes reflex, not recall.

3. COMMIT TO MISSIONAL COMMUNITY

Isolation kills momentum. Evangelism thrives in community. You need people who will pray with you, encourage you, and challenge you to keep going.

A missional community isn't just a Bible study; it's a launch pad. A group of believers who gather regularly to pray for the lost, share stories, and hold each other accountable to live on mission.

When I was in college, I met weekly with a small group at 6 a.m. We'd pray, train, and then go out into our city to share our faith. It changed everything. Accountability made us brave; encouragement made it fun.

Research confirms this. In *Spiritual Multiplication in the Real World*, Bob McNabb found that believers in missional communities share their faith far more consistently than those who go solo. Boldness grows best in groups.

Next Step: Don't wait for one to start, create one. Find 2–3 people in your church or youth group ready to *live loud*, and meet weekly to pray, practice accountability, and share stories.

4. MEMORIZE CONVERSATION STARTERS

The hardest part of evangelism isn't sharing the gospel; it's starting the conversation. That first word can feel like a mountain. But you don't need clever lines, you just need courage and curiosity.

Simple questions can open eternal doors:

- "How are you really doing?"
- "Do you have any spiritual beliefs?"
- "Can I tell you something that changed my life?"

My conversation with Breanna in Chapter 2 started with three simple words: "How are you?" And it led to a life-changing discussion about faith.

Once, after a pickup basketball game, I felt prompted to bring up Jesus to a group of teens. I hesitated, then remembered the question: "Do you have any spiritual beliefs?" Minutes later, we were sitting on the court, and two students prayed to receive Christ.

Don't underestimate the power of a question; it's the key that unlocks the heart.

Next Step: Choose two conversation starters and memorize them. The next time you sense the Spirit nudging you, use one.

5. LEARN EVANGELISM METHODS

Methods don't save people, Jesus does. But tools help you explain the message clearly and confidently.

Think of methods as maps; they guide the conversation while keeping the focus on Christ. Here are a few worth mastering:

- The Three Circles – illustrates God's design, our brokenness, and Jesus' redemption.

- The Romans Road – walks through key verses that explain salvation.

- Five Share Jesus Questions – helps you guide conversations naturally.

And don't forget your testimony. It's the most personal gospel story you'll ever tell. Keep it simple:

1. Who you were before Christ.

2. When you surrendered your life to Him.

3. How has your life changed since?

Then ask, "Do you have a story like mine?"

Next Step: Practice sharing your story in under three minutes. Use one of these methods to make the gospel clear, not complicated.

6. MASTER A TRANSITION STATEMENT

The key to sharing your faith isn't forcing conversations; it's flowing into them naturally.

Jimmy Scroggins says, "A good transition statement is the key." When someone shares about pain, anxiety, or uncertainty, that's a Spirit-prompted moment. A simple line like:

"Can I share something with you that's really helped me?"

It's the bridge between their story and God's story. Practice saying it aloud. It might feel awkward at first, but soon it will become part of your rhythm. One well-timed sentence can turn a casual chat into a gospel conversation.

Next Step: Write two transition statements that feel natural for you. Say them out loud until they sound like you.

7. ALWAYS GIVE AN INVITATION

The gospel demands a response. Don't just drop truth and walk away; invite people to take a step. You might ask:

"What's holding you back from placing your faith in Jesus today?"

If they're ready, walk them through Romans 10:9–10:

> *"If you confess with your mouth that Jesus is Lord and believe in your heart that God raised Him from the dead, you will be saved."*

Lead them in prayer, but remind them: it's not the prayer that saves—Jesus does. The prayer simply gives voice to belief.

Some will say no. Some will say not yet. But others will say yes—and heaven will celebrate.

Next Step: Make it your goal this month to not just share the gospel, but to invite. Give someone the opportunity to respond.

FINAL THOUGHT

None of these habits replaces the power of the Holy Spirit; they simply make room for Him to move.

Preparation doesn't produce revival, but it prepares the soil for it. When you're intentional with your list, your Scripture, your community, your questions, and your invitations, you become a vessel ready for God's use.

Evangelism isn't about perfection; it's about availability.

Write some names down. Memorize the verses. Gather your community. Ask the questions. Share your story. Offer the invitation.

And then stand back and watch what God does when ordinary believers start living loud with extraordinary confidence.

REFLECTION QUESTIONS

1. Which part of this list do you practice consistently? Which one do you neglect?

2. Who are three people you would add to your Reach List right now, and how can you begin praying for them?

    _____

    _____

    _____

    _____

3. How confident do you feel sharing the gospel from memory? Which verse from this chapter will you commit to memorizing first?

    _____

    _____

    _____

    _____

4. What simple conversation starter could you practice this week to break the ice with someone?

    _____

    _____

    _____

    _____

5. Why is it important not only to share the gospel but also to extend an invitation?

    _____

    _____

ACTION STEPS

- Create your Reach List. Write down 3–5 names today and commit to praying for them daily this week.

- Memorize one new gospel verse (Romans 3:23, Romans 6:23, John 3:16, etc.) so you're ready to share it.

- Practice your transition statement aloud until it feels natural: "Can I share something with you that has really helped me?"

- Extend one clear invitation to someone this week after sharing the gospel.

"The Great Commission begins with the person closest to you."
– Unknown

CHAPTER 10:
YOUR MISSION FIELD
HAS A NAME

"Go home to your own people and tell them how much the Lord has done for you, and how he has had mercy on you."
– Mark 5:19

As we close this book, I want to pause and say something few people hear often enough: I'm proud of you.

Most people would have closed this book chapters ago, convinced that living loud was too costly, too inconvenient, or too intimidating. But not you. You stayed. You reflected. You prayed. You wrestled with what it means to break the silence and embrace bold faith.

And now here we are, the finish line that isn't really a finish line at all because the end of this book is the beginning of your mission.

The question is no longer, *"Why should I share my faith?"* It's now, *"Where do I start?"*

START SMALL. START CLOSE.

Personal evangelism can feel overwhelming when we think about reaching "the whole world." But Jesus never told us to start with the globe; He told us to start with our neighbors.

Greg Laurie puts it well:

> "We should shift Jesus' command from 'Go into all the world' to 'Go into all your world.'"

Your world is your classroom, your office, your neighborhood, your team, your family, your friend group. It's the coffee shop you spend way too much money at, the gym you go to, and even the sidelines where your kids play. It's the cashier you see weekly, the coworker in the next cubicle, the relative who still doesn't understand your faith.

That's where living loud begins.

Jesus modeled this principle perfectly in **Mark 5:19**, speaking to the man healed from demon possession:

> *"Go home to your own people and tell them how much the Lord has done for you."*

He didn't tell him to cross oceans or preach in distant synagogues. He told him to start where he was, with those he knew.

You don't have to go far to *live loud.* You just have to go faithful.

SHINE WHERE YOU ARE

Your circles— the places, people, and routines of your life are your mission field. You don't need a platform, an invitation, or the perfect words. What you need is faithfulness. Every step of faith in your "world" counts. Every story told, every prayer whispered, every invitation given—these are eternal investments.

CLASSMATES

Students carry enormous influence among peers. Walk through your school's hallways, and you'll hear it—conversations about anxiety, heartbreak, confusion, and identity. Behind every laugh, every hoodie, is a heart searching for hope.

Here's the beautiful truth: God placed you there on purpose.

You may not have a pulpit, but you do have a platform. Your classroom, lunch table, study group, or sports team is your mission field. The greatest person to reach a teenager is another teenager unashamed of their faith.

Start small: pray before tests, share your testimony at lunch, invite friends to youth group. Bring another believer with you so you're not alone. And if classmates ever whisper, *"You're one of those Jesus people,"* smile. You're not being weird; you're being set apart.

When life falls apart for those around you (and it will), they'll remember who stood strong. Be that person.

COWORKERS

For those in the workplace, your mission field is often across the desk, not across the ocean. It's easy to think evangelism belongs to preachers and missionaries, but for many of us, it happens in break rooms, after meetings, and during carpool conversations. Lunch breaks, coffee runs, or casual moments are ripe for relational evangelism.

A key note: relational evangelism must eventually point to the gospel. Shane Pruitt wisely says:

"Relational evangelism eventually has to get to the point where we're actually sharing the gospel in our relationships. Otherwise, we're just friending people all the way to Hell."

Be intentional with the relationships you build, asking genuine questions like:

- "What's your story?"
- "What's been giving you purpose lately?"
- "How can I pray for you?"

Even if your workplace discourages religious talk, you can always share your story. People can debate theology, but they cannot argue with your transformation.

Model integrity. Show compassion. Let your work ethic and kindness make your faith believable. Jesus met people in fishing boats and at dinner tables; you can meet Him in boardrooms and break rooms.

TEAMMATES

Teams are families forged by sweat, competition, and shared goals. You celebrate victories together and mourn losses together. That camaraderie builds trust—and trust builds open doors.

Tim Tebow once said:

> "God wants to use you where you are with what you have. Not just in the future when you get to where you think you want to go, but now."

Don't wait until you feel "ready." Ministry rarely happens in ideal moments. Use car rides, bus trips, and locker rooms to bring hope into everyday life. Pray before games. Encourage teammates who are struggling. Celebrate wins with humility and handle losses with grace.

God placed you on that team for more than stats on a scoreboard. You're there for souls.

FAMILY

Family is often the hardest mission field, and the most necessary. You didn't choose your family, but God placed you in it for a reason.

Maybe you're the only believer in your household. Maybe you have a skeptical sibling, a distant parent, or a relative who's drifted. Evangelism at home requires patience, gentleness, and prayer. The gospel should never skip your own household. Love your family well by giving them the greatest gift, the truth about Christ.

Start with honest, humble conversations:

- "What do you think heaven is like?"

- "Have you ever wondered what faith means to me?"

- "Can I share something Jesus has done in my life?"

Consistency matters. Sometimes your family doesn't need a sermon; they need an example. Live your faith at home with love, not lectures. Be patient with their process.

FRIENDS

Friends are gifts from God. They laugh with you, cry with you, and walk through life by your side. But real love doesn't stay silent about eternity. If you wouldn't hide a life-saving cure from your best friend, why would you hide the gospel?

Start conversations that go deeper:

- "Where do you find peace when life gets hard?"
- "Do you ever think about eternity?"
- "What do you believe about Jesus?"

You don't need to preach, just share. Share how you met Christ. Share what He's done for you. Share the difference He's made.

Real love risks awkward moments for the sake of eternal ones. Imagine the joy of seeing your friends not only as companions in life but as brothers and sisters in Christ.

STRANGERS

Every person you encounter is a divine appointment. Think about this: the average person walks over 75,000 miles in their lifetime. That's thousands of opportunities to cross paths with someone who needs Jesus.

Evangelism isn't confined to mission trips; it's woven into everyday moments: the cashier at Target, the Uber driver, the server at lunch, the parent sitting next to you at your kid's soccer game.

You never know what small act of kindness or short word of truth might plant a seed in someone's heart.

I'll never forget a mission trip to Miami when our group practiced street evangelism at a local mall. Before sharing, we prayed. Afterwards, three teenage boys wandered over. We struck up a casual conversation, asked about their beliefs, and shared the gospel. Two mocked us, but one, Jaidyn, leaned in. He listened intently, thanked us, and even connected on social media.

A year later, Jaidyn messaged me:

> *"DUDE. This is insane. I was in church with my girlfriend last Sunday, and I thought about what really got me into God. I remembered that rainy day at the mall when you stopped me before my basketball game. That one conversation changed my life. I pray every day now. You have no idea how much you impacted me. You're somebody I'm going to tell my kids about one day."*

One conversation. One moment of boldness. And eternity shifted.

Even when you feel like it's not working; God's working.

That's what happens when you *live loud*; you never know whose eternity you'll impact.

THE GOAL

The goal of breaking free from silent Christianity isn't just turning up the volume of your faith; it's giving unbelievers a chance to hear the gospel and respond.

Here's a challenge: fill in this blank:

I will share the gospel with _____.

That blank represents more than a goal; it represents a soul. It may look simple, but it's where transformation begins. As you apply the strategies and principles in this book, I hope that you won't just check off an evangelism task, but you'll celebrate changed lives.

But obedience requires practice. Evangelism is a spiritual muscle that grows stronger with exercise. The more we use it, the more natural it becomes. Christians who share their faith aren't radical; they're simply returning to what normal Christianity should look like.

When you love someone deeply, you don't hesitate to talk about them. You speak freely because love overflows. That's what happens when your heart burns for Jesus. The more you fall in love with Him, the more naturally you'll speak about Him. Evangelism stops being a burden and becomes the overflow of a heart that truly knows Christ.

A FINAL COMMISSION

Here's the question as you close this book: What will change?

Will your classmates know where to find hope? Will coworkers hear your story? Will teammates see faith in action? Will your family sense a shift toward Christ-centered conversations? Will your friends finally hear the truth from your lips? Will strangers encounter grace through your kindness and courage?

You don't have to reach everyone; you just have to reach someone. You don't need to have it all figured out; you just need to take the next step. Maybe that means sending a text right now that says, "You free to talk today?" That single act of obedience could open the door to eternity.

This is your invitation to *live loud*; not someday, but today. Not perfectly, but passionately. Not waiting for permission, but walking in power.

Because the same Spirit that raised Jesus from the dead now lives in you. The same God who used fishermen, tax collectors, and shepherds wants to use students, parents, entrepreneurs, and everyday believers to carry His name to the world. You are part of that story. You are God's plan A, and there is no plan B.

I pray this book hasn't just been ink on paper but a spark in your soul, a divine interruption that calls you out of comfort and into courage. Imagine what could happen if believers everywhere decided to break the silence and turn the volume up. Imagine neighborhoods, schools, workplaces, and families where Jesus isn't whispered but declared with love and boldness.

It starts with one conversation. One act of obedience. One prayer whispered in faith. From that spark, revival spreads.

So, rise up. Speak up. *Live loud.* Let your life be the microphone that amplifies the mercy of God.

The world doesn't need quieter Christians; it needs courageous ones. And you, reader, are called to be one of them.

Hobby Lobby was the place where I realized silence costs souls. But it was also the place God began stirring this message in me, that faith was never meant to whisper.

Wherever you go from here, remember: the same Spirit who nudged me that day is nudging you right now.

Don't hold back. Don't stay quiet.

It's time to *live loud.*

REFLECTION QUESTIONS

1. Which sphere of influence, classmates, coworkers, teammates, family, friends, or strangers, do you find most challenging to engage with the gospel? Why?

2. Who is one person in your proximity you've been avoiding when it comes to sharing Jesus? What's holding you back?

3. How does Jaidyn's story challenge your view of "ordinary" conversations with strangers?

4. Which practical step from this chapter could you take this week to make your faith louder in your world?

5. If every Christian in your circle intentionally lived out this chapter, how would your school, workplace, or community look different?

ACTION STEPS

- Write your circles. Take a piece of paper and list five names for each category: classmates, coworkers, teammates, family, friends, and strangers you encounter regularly.

- Start small. Choose one name from your list and reach out this week, send a text, invite them for coffee, or have a simple gospel conversation.

- Share your testimony. Practice telling your story to a friend or family member, then ask, "Do you have a story like mine?"

- Pray for boldness. Ask God daily to give you the courage and confidence to interrupt silence in the circles where He's placed you.

.

JOIN THE MOVEMENT

Live Loud isn't just a book; it's a calling.

It's for every believer tired of a quiet faith and ready to live unashamed.

If God has used these pages to stir something in your heart, I'd love to help you keep growing in boldness.

Text LOUD to 601-616-0059 (my personal number) and you'll receive:

- A free *"Share Your Faith Toolkit"* to help you start gospel conversations
- Practical ways to live out what you've read
- & encouragement from me and others choosing to *live loud* across the world

When believers *live loud*, people notice. Yet it's not about being noticed; it's about helping others notice the goodness of God.

Let's be the generation that refuses to stay silent.

— **Anthony Vargas**

ONE FINAL STORY

Now, I know you picked up a nonfiction book, but for a moment, let's imagine.

It's the year 2052. Christianity is outlawed. The underground church has gone quiet. The Kill Every Christian movement has nearly completed its mission. Nearly, because there's still one follower of Jesus left.

You.

The world has changed. Streets are empty. Crosses that once stood tall above cities have been torn down and replaced with digital billboards preaching a new kind of god, 'self'. The name of Jesus, once sung in stadiums and shouted from pulpits, now survives only in secret. Bibles are burned. Churches lie in ruins. The gospel has become a crime.

The world moves faster but grows darker. Artificial light fills every corner, except the human heart. Hope feels extinct. The sound of worship is gone. But somewhere, in the silence, one flame still flickers.

One believer still believes.

One voice still speaks.

Yours.

You hide during the day. You move by night. Every prayer is a risk. Every whisper of the Word could mean death. And yet, something inside you burns louder than fear.

You remember what He said: "Go into all the world."

So you do. Quietly. Boldly. One conversation at a time.

The world may have outlawed your faith, but it cannot outlaw your voice.

If the survival of Christianity rested on your faith, your courage, your obedience—would it become extinct?

Coming Soon: One Last Christian

A work of fiction inspired by truth.

Step into a future where faith is forbidden, the Bible is banned, and the Church has gone silent. The gospel is now a crime, whispered only in the dark. Across a broken world where belief has been erased, one follower of Jesus remains— hunted, hidden, but unshaken.

This is the story of:

- Courage when hope is outlawed
- Conviction when fear reigns
- One believer who refuses to stop sharing the name that can still save them all

In a time when Christianity is just a memory, one voice will remind the world that light still breaks through the darkness.

One Last Christian — a novel coming soon.

Because even in the end, the gospel can't be stopped.